ENGLISH PLEASE!

English for the Arab World
BOOK 2

by Richard Harrison

CONTENTS

Pearson Education Limited
Edinburgh Gate, Harlow,
Essex CM20 2JE, England
and Associated Companies throughout the world

www.longman.com

Addison Wesley Longman Limited 1996

First published 1996
Seventh impression 2002

Set in 12/15pt Avant Garde

Printed in China
GCC/07

ISBN 0 582 21707 5

Introduction - To the Student

Welcome to Book 2 of *English Please!* a new English course for the Arab World. The course consists of a Starter Book, Book 1 and Book 2.

In Book 2 you will learn to do these things in English:

- give people information about your-self
- describe where you live and where you work
- write your address
- tell the time
- offer drinks and food to visitors
- read a menu in English
- order food in a restaurant
- talk about your likes and dislikes
- ask about the price of something
- tell people about your daily life
- tell people about the daily life of friends or relatives
- describe what is happening at the moment
- tell people where you are going
- talk about the weather
- give instructions to other people

You will learn a lot of new words to do with - food, drink, clothes, the weather, office furniture, school subjects, colours, jobs, relatives, animals, months of the year, hobbies, etc. Try to learn these words and practise using them in sentences.

You will also learn a little about the grammar of English and how to write sentences, simple paragraphs and short letters to friends.

تقديم إلى الطالب

مرحبًا بك معنا في سلسلة الكتاب الثاني *English Please!*، و هو سلسلة جديدة في اللغة الإنجليزية لطلبة العالم العربي .

تتكون هذه السلسلة من كتاب أولي بالإضافة إلى كتابين : الأول و الثاني .

في الكتاب الثاني سوف يتعلم الطالب كيف يؤدي ما يلي باللغة الإنجليزية :

– إعطاء الناس معلومات عن نفسه .

– وصف مكان إقامته ، و مكان عمله .

– كتابة عنوانه .

– التعريف بالوقت .

–عرض تقديم الشراب و الطعام للزائرين .

– قراءة قائمة الطعام .

– طلب الطعام في مطعم .

– الحديث عما يحب و عما يكره .

– السؤال عن سعر سلعة .

– محادثة الناس عن حياته اليومية .

– محادثة الناس عن حياة الأصدقاء أو الأقارب اليومية .

– وصف ما يحدث في اللحظة الحالية .

– إبلاغ الناس إلى أين سيذهب .

– الحديث عن الطقس .

– إصدار التعليمات

سوف يتعلم الطالب أيضًا كلمات جديدة عن : الطعام ، و الشراب ، و الملابس ، و الطقس ، و أثاث المكتب ، و المواد الدراسية ، و الألوان ، و الوظائف ، و الأقارب ، و الحيوانات ، و شهور السنة ، و الهوايات ، إلخ . و سوف يحاول أن يتعلمها و يستخدمها في جمل.

بالإضافة إلى ذلك سوف يتعلم الطالب القليل من قواعد اللغة الإنجليزية ، و كيف يكون جملاً ، و فقرات بسيطة ، و كيف يكتب رسائل قصيرة للأصدقاء .

Book 2 is divided into these parts:

Students' Book
Workbook
Appendix

The Workbook is an important part of the course. At the end of every lesson in the Students' Book you should turn to that lesson in the Workbook.

By the end of the *English Please!* course you should be able to communicate with people in English. This means you can speak to those people who speak English as their first language, for example, British and Americans, and also to people such as Japanese, Filipinos, Swedes and Indians, who have learned English as a second language. Practise your English with them when you can. Good luck!

وينقسم الكتاب الثاني إلى الأجزاء الآتية :

كتاب التلميذ .

كراسة الأعمال التحريرية .

الملحق .

وكراسة الأعمال التحريرية جزء مهم في هذه السلسلة . و في نهاية كل درس ، في كتاب التلميذ ، يجب على الطالب أن يرجع إلى الدرس نفسه في كراسة الأعمال التحريرية .

بنهاية سلسلة *English Please!* ، يمكنك التخاطب مع الآخرين باللغة الإنجليزية ؛ أي يمكنك أن تخاطب الأشخاص الذين يتحدثون الإنجليزية كلغة أولى ، مثل البريطانيين و الأمريكيين ، و كذلك اليابانيين و الفيليبينيين و السويديين و الهنود الذين يتعلمون الإنجليزية كلغة ثانية . مارس الحديث معهم باللغة الإنجليزية قدر المستطاع .

حظًا سعيدًا !

UNIT 1 AT WORK

Lesson 1 A new job

1 Listen and write

Write **A**, **B** or **C**.

A

Where are you from, Saleem?
I'm from Taif.
Is that near Riyadh?
No, it isn't. It's near Jeddah.

B

Have you got a driving licence?
Well, I've got a British driving licence.
Yes, but have you got a Jordanian licence?
No, I haven't.

C

Where were you born, Mr Patel?
I was born in Poona.
Poona? Where's that?
It's in India, not far from Bombay.

2 Listen and say

Where are you from?

Where were you born?

Where's that?

Have you got a driving licence?

3 Read

Have you got a ...?

work permit

passport

driving licence

visa

certificate

diploma

4 Ask and answer

A

Have you got a driving licence?

B

Yes, I have.
No, I haven't.

5 Listen and say

Say the "**dr**" sound.

driving licence, ad**dr**ess, hun**dr**ed, be**dr**oom, **dr**ink

Language

Where were you born?
I was born in ...

Have you got a ...?
Yes, I have.
No, I haven't.

| Lesson 2 | What's your address? |

1 Listen

Ahmed: What's your address, Mr Robertson?
Jim: My address? It's ... P.O. Box 50.
Ahmed: P.O. Box 15.
Jim: No. 50 not 15.
Ahmed: Oh. P.O. Box 50.
Jim: Adliya.
Ahmed: How do you spell that?
Jim: A...D...L...I...Y...A.
Ahmed: Adliya. Yes. And where's that?
Jim: It's a suburb of Manama.
Ahmed: Manama. And that's in Bahrain?
Jim: Yes.

2 Write

Complete the envelope.

Mr Jim Robertson
P.O. Box _____ ,

_____ ,

Manama,

_____ .

[stamp 41']

Look!

P.O. Box = Post Office Box

3 Match

Write the words under the pictures: **stamp, letter, address, envelope**

4 Listen and say

What's your address?

What's your telephone number?

What's your date of birth?

5 Read

1st, 2nd, 3rd, 4th, 5th, 6th, 7th, 8th, 9th, 10th

6 Listen and say

Months:

January, February, March, April, May, June

Look!

Date

4th January 1995 = 4/1/95

(the fourth of January nineteen ninety-five)

7 Listen and write

Put these words in the correct list.

address, fifteen, suburb, licence, passport, between, hotel, fifty

morning   today

_____   _____

_____   _____

_____   _____

_____   _____

Language

What's your address?	*Dates*
My address is ...	*Months:* January, February, March, April, May, June

---

Lesson 3   This is our office

1 Read

Mary has a new job.

This is our office, Mary.

It's nice.

Yes. And this is your desk.

And that's your chair.

And is this my computer?

No, That's Salwa's

That's yours – over there.

Oh. I see.

2 Match

Match the words with the pictures:

typewriter, cupboard, chair, desk, computer, shelf, filing cabinet, table

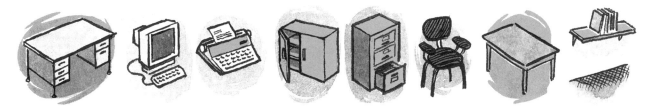

3 Listen and say

Months : **July, August, September, October, November, December**

Dates : **11th, 12th, 13th, 14th, 15th, 16th, 17th, 18th, 19th, 20th**

4 Match

Write the words under the pictures: **cap, hat, uniform, overalls**

5 Write

Write in these words: **next, Waleed's, over, yours, where's, your**

A: That's (a) _____ locker, Samir.

B: I see. Thanks. And is this my uniform?

A: No, that's (b) _____. This is (c) _____, here.

B: Right. And (d) _____ my cap?

A: It's (e) _____ there, (f) _____ to the door.

6 Listen and say

Sentence stress

a) That's **my** computer, not **yours**.

b) No, My bag's not **blue**, it's **black**.

c) I was born in **March** not **May**.

d) She's not from **Jordan**. She's from **Lebanon**.

e) My name's **Samir** not **Samira**!

Lesson 4   Show me your pass, please

1 Listen

Guard: Show me your pass, please.
Bob: I'm sorry. I haven't got one.
Guard: Oh! Well, have you got an identification card?
Bob: No I haven't. But I've got a driving licence.
Guard: Can I see it?
Bob: Yes, here you are.
Guard: Thank you. Wait here a minute, please.

2 Write

a) Bob hasn't got a _____.

b) He hasn't got an _____.

c) Bob has got a _____.

Look!

Show me ... / Can I see ...?

Show me your pass,   please.
                 passport,
                 driving licence,

Can I see your pass, please?

3 Ask and answer

A	B
Show me ..., please.	Yes, here you are.
Can I see ..., please?	I'm sorry. I haven't got a ...

4 Match

NO ENTRY

SLOW

STOP

DANGER

NO SMOKING

NO PARKING

5 Read

21st, 22nd, 23rd, 24th ... 30th, 31st

twenty-first, twenty-second, twenty-third, twenty-fourth ... thirtieth, thirty-first

6 Read the dates

a) 1st November 1995
b) 12/4/96
c) 26th July 1980
d) 3rd Oct. '94
e) 21/5/98
f) 2nd Jan. 1997

7 Listen and say

Say the "o" sound.

Oh!, show, slow, go, no, phone, smoking, road, don't, know

Language

Dates: 21st–31st

Show me ...
Can I see ...?

Here you are.

9

was/were

Present		Past
I am	–	I was
You are	–	You were

Where *were* you born?   I *was* born in ...

Have you got a ...?   Yes, I have.
                       No, I haven't.

---

my/mine

It's	my ...	mine		our ...	ours
	your ...	yours		your ...	yours
	his ...	his		their ...	theirs
	her ...	hers			

"Is this *my* desk?"   "No, that's *mine*. That's *yours* over there."
"Is that *her* filing cabinet?"   "No, it isn't *hers*. It's *ours*."
"Is that *Salwa's* computer?"   "No, this is *Salwa's*, here."

Show me ...,   please.
Can I see ...,   please?

Yes. Here you are.

Dates

31/10/73	=	31st Oct. 1973	=	the thirty-first of October, nineteen seventy-three
23/4/94	=	23rd April 1994	=	the twenty-third of April, nineteen ninety-four
2/1/2001	=	2nd Jan. 2001	=	the second of January, two thousand and one

---

What's your   address?
               telephone number?
               date of birth?

NEW WORDS

Learn these words:

Office vocabulary
filing cabinet
typewriter
address
envelope
stamp
shelf/shelves
computer

Countries
India
Canada
Pakistan

Nationalities
Indian
Jordan
British

Months
January
February
March
April
May
June
July
August
September
October
November
December

Clothes
hat
cap
overalls
uniform

Verbs
wait
show

Documents
pass
work permit
document
certificate
diploma
identification card
driving licence

Others
suburb
district
date of birth
main gate
guard
slow
at work

_____

_____

_____

_____

_____

_____

_____

_____

_____

_____

UNIT 2 AT HOME

Lesson 1   Please come in

1 Read

2 Match

Write the words under the pictures:

coffee, sugar, tea, a sandwich, a cake

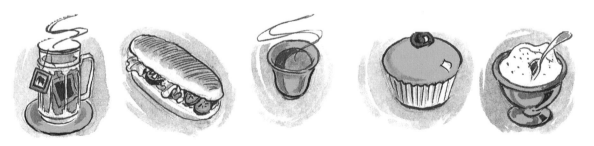

Look!

some / a

Would you like **some** tea?

Would you like **a** biscuit?

Would you like **some** biscuits?

3 Listen and say

Would you like some tea?

Would you like a biscuit?

Have a sandwich.

Look!

Saying "Yes":   **Yes,** please.
Thank you.

Saying "No":   **No,** thank you.
No, thanks.

4 Ask and answer

A	B
Would you like a/some ...?	Yes, please.
Have a/some ...	No, thank you.
	No, thanks.

5 Listen and say

Sounds and spelling.

"**sss**" and "**sh**"

sss: **s**peak, **s**ay, **s**it down, ye**s**, poli**ce**, ni**ce**, **c**ity, pala**ce**

sh: **s**ugar, **sh**e, pu**sh**, **sh**op, na**ti**onality, deli**ci**ous, mousta**che**

6 Listen and say

Listen and say the weak forms of these words:

a) some, a, of, you, to, for
b) some tea, a cup of tea, would you like, to Mary, it's for you
c) Would you like some tea?
   Can I speak to Mary?

7 Listen

Sounds and spelling.

bis**cui**t, b**ui**lding
j**ui**ce, s**ui**tcase

Would you like orange juice or lemonade?

Language

Would you like ...?
Have a ...

some/a some tea, a biscuit

Yes, Please.
No, thank you.

It's delicious. They're delicious.

at home

1   Listen and write

Write **A, B, C,** or **D**.

A

Ahmed:	Some more coffee, Sam?
Sam:	No thanks.
Ahmed:	Well, have another cake.
Sam:	No. They're delicious, but I'm full.

B

Latifa:	Would you like some fruit?
Sarah:	Yes, I would.
Latifa:	Help yourself.
Sarah:	Thanks. I think I'll have an apple.

C

Fatima:	How's the coffee?
Tom:	It's fine thanks.
Mary:	Can I have some milk, please?
Fatima:	Of course. Here you are.
Mary:	Thanks. That's enough.

D

Hassan:	Have some more meat.
Jim:	Yes. I'd like some more.
Hassan:	And would you like some more salad?
Jim:	No thanks. I've got enough.

2   Match

Match the words with the pictures: **meat, rice, salad, bread, chicken**

3   Ask and answer

Offer your guest **some more** : rice, meat, bread, salad, ice-cream, chicken
      or   **another** : cake, biscuit, apple, orange, cup of coffee, sandwich

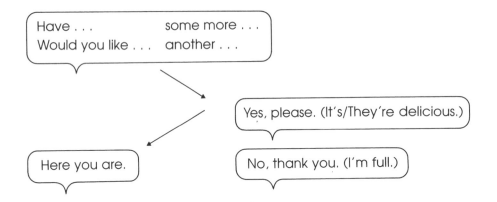

Have . . .   some more . . .
Would you like . . . another . . .

Yes, please. (It's/They're delicious.)

Here you are.

No, thank you. (I'm full.)

4   Look and say

What would these people like? Make sentences with: **I'd like ...**

5 Write

Write in these words: **I'd, full, another, some, here, of course, thanks, have, down, would**

Mike: Please sit (a) _____, Jameel.

Jameel: Thanks.

Mike: Would you like (b) _____ orange juice?

Jameel: Yes, I (c) _____. I'm very thirsty.

Mike: (d) _____ you are.

Jameel: Thanks.

Fatima: (e) _____ some dates, Mary. They're sweet.

Mary: No (f) _____.

Fatima: Or would you like (g) _____ cake?

Mary: No, really. I'm quite (h) _____. But (I) _____ like a glass of water.

Fatima: (j) _____. Just a minute.

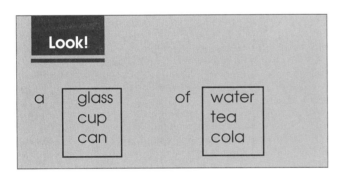

a	glass cup can	of water tea cola

6 Act it out!

A You are at home. Welcome your guests. Give them food and drink.
B You are a guest. You are hot and thirsty, but you are not hungry.
C You are a guest. You are hot and thirsty, and you are also quite hungry.

7 Listen and say

Say the "I" sound.

I, I'd, like, m**y**, mine, **i**ce-cream, five, **I**rish, good-b**y**e, time, dining room

8 Listen

Sounds and spelling.

guest, **gu**ard, **g**ot, **g**as, **g**oal, **g**lass, **g**arage

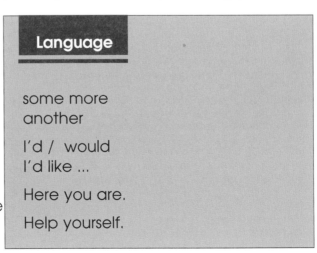

Language

some more
another

I'd / would
I'd like ...

Here you are.

Help yourself.

Lesson 3   I like hot weather

1   Listen

Bashir:	Come in, Peter.
Peter:	Thanks.
Bashir:	This is my brother, Waleed.
Peter:	How do you do?
Waleed:	Pleased to meet you.
Bashir:	Have a seat. Would you like a cold drink, Peter? There's cola, orange...
Peter:	Have you got any lemonade?
Bashir:	Lemonade? Yes. Here you are.
Peter:	Thanks. That's good. Isn't it hot today?
Waleed:	Yes, very. But I like hot weather.
Peter:	Do you? I don't. I like cold weather. I like Bahrain in the winter.
Bashir:	Me too. Have some more lemonade, Peter.
Peter:	Thanks.

Look!

Like

I **like** cold weather.
I **don't like** hot weather.
Do you like hot weather?

don't = do not

I don't speak French.
I do not speak French.

Which is Peter's drink?

2 Write

Write these sentences with *don't*.

a)   I like football very much. (table-tennis) _____

b)   I know her name. (address) _____

c)   I understand French. (German) _____

d)   I have a job. (a house) _____

e)   I speak English very well. (Urdu) _____

3 Look and say

I like ... (very much).   I don't like ...

4 Ask and answer

Now ask another student about the pictures above.

      A   **B**

Do you like ...?   No, I don't.
                   Yes, I do.

> **Look!**
>
> *any*
>
> Have you got **any** lemonade?
> I haven't got **any** petrol.
> I haven't got **any** biscuits.
>
> I've got **some** water.
> I've got **some** cakes.

5 Listen and say

Say the "**O**" sound

Oh!, n**o**, d**o**n't g**o**, c**o**ld, s**o**, bel**ow**

Say the "**o**" sound:

h**o**t, g**o**t, n**o**t, j**o**b, st**o**p, w**a**tch, cl**o**ck

6 Listen and tick (✓)

a) ☐ got ☐ goat
b) ☐ got ☐ goat
c) ☐ got ☐ goat
d) ☐ got ☐ goat

e) ☐ not ☐ note
f) ☐ not ☐ note
g) ☐ not ☐ note
h) ☐ not ☐ note

7 Listen and say

Sounds and spelling.

r**ea**d, pl**ea**se, t**ea**cher, r**ea**lly, n**ea**r
w**ea**ther, br**ea**d, h**ea**d

Language

I like ...
I don't like ... (+ a noun)
Do you like ...?

some/ any

in the winter, in the summer

Lesson 4   I like cooking

1 Listen

Sarah: Do you like cooking, Latifa?
Latifa: Yes, I do. I like it very much. Do you?
Sarah: No. Not much.
Latifa: Why not?
Sarah: Because it's difficult.
Latifa: Difficult? No, it isn't. It is easy. I'll teach you.
Sarah: OK.
Latifa: Look. This is "foul medames".
Sarah: What?
Latifa: "Foul medames". It's an Egyptian dish.
Sarah: What is it in English?
Latifa: I'm not sure. Beans, I think.
Sarah: Hmmm. I like beans.
Latifa: Good. Well, the first thing is ...

a)   What is foul medames in English?
b)   Where is foul medames from?

20

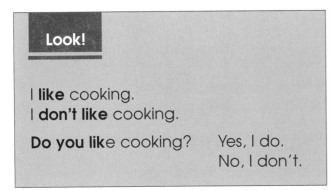

Look!

I **like** cooking.
I **don't like** cooking.

Do you like cooking? Yes, I do.
No, I don't.

Look!

-ing

I like   cook**ing**.
        read**ing**.
        learn**ing** English.
        driv**ing**.

VERB		+	-ING		
cook		+	-ing	=	cooking
read		+	-ing	=	reading
learn		+	-ing	=	learning
drive ('e')		+	-ing	=	driving

2 Listen and say

Do you like: cooking?
              reading?
              driving?

              learning English?
              watching television?

3 Ask and answer

Ask another student.

A	**B**	
Do you like ... (cooking)?	Yes, I do.	No, I don't.
	Yes, I like ... very much.	No. Not much.

4 Match

Write these words under the pictures: **walking, reading, swimming, watching TV, learning English, driving, fishing, cooking, shopping.**

_____ _____ _____ _____ _____

_____ _____ _____ _____

5 Match

It's ... **difficult/easy/interesting.**

6 Write

Write in these words: **much, very, don't, interesting, because, do, driving, too, why, like**

A: (a) _____ you like (b) _____ , Ahmed?

B: No. Not (c) _____ .

A: Why not?

B: (d) _____ there are a lot of cars on the road.

C: I (e) _____ reading very much.

D: Me (f) _____ . It's very (g) _____ .

C: But I (h) _____ like watching television.

D: (i) _____ not?

C: Because the programmes aren't (j) _____ good.

7 Listen and say

Say these **-ing** words:

cooking, morning, evening, dining room, sitting room, single, shopping, spelling, thing, interesting

The Present Simple Tense

I like ...	Do you like ...?	I don't speak English.
I don't like ...	I speak English.	Do you speak English?

---

ing *forms*   Verb +   -ing
                      cook +   - ing   =   cooking

I like cooking. I don't like driving. Do you like playing basketball?

Would

Would you like ...? Yes, I would.   I'd like ...

Have ...

Have   a seat.   some fruit.   another cup of coffee.

---

come in   go out   sit down   stand up

Saying "Yes":	Yes, please.	Saying "No":	No, thanks.
	Thank you.		No, thank you.

Countable/ Uncountable nouns

Uncountable nouns: water, tea, rice, bread, milk
I'd like some tea.
I'd like some more tea.

Countable nouns: biscuit, cake, date, apple

I'd like a biscuit.
I'd like some biscuits.
I'd like another biscuit.
I'd like some more biscuits

Some/any

I've got some nice biscuits.   I haven't got any bread.
Have you got any milk?

Why do you like cooking?   Because it's interesting.
Why ...? Because ...

NEW WORDS

Learn these words:

Food	Drink	Adjectives	Other
chicken	lemonade	interesting	summer
meat	milk	easy	winter
beans	cola	difficult	weather
bread	water	delicious	glass
sugar	(a) drink		can
cake			cup
biscuit			dish
			goat

verbs (-ing)	Verb		note
cooking	to like		at home
driving			help yourself
walking			enough
swimming			the first thing
watching			
learning			
playing			
visiting			
fishing			
shopping			

_____   _____

_____   _____

_____   _____

_____   _____

_____   _____

_____   _____

_____   _____

Review Unit A

GRAMMAR

1 Write

Present	Past
I am	I was
you are	you were

Write **am** (**'m**), **are**, **was** or **were** in the spaces.

A: Where (a) _____ you from, Tariq?

B: I (b) _____ from Lahore in Pakistan.

A: (c) _____ you born in Pakistan?

B: No. I (d) _____ born in Delhi in India.

A: So what's your nationality? (e) _____ you Indian?

B: No. I (f) _____ Pakistani.

2 Write

Countable	a	biscuit	some biscuits
	an	orange	some oranges
Uncountable		some tea	
		some sugar	

Write **a**, **an** or **some** in the spaces.

Have _____ dates.

I think I'll have _____ banana.

Would you like _____ coffee?

_____ more rice?

I'd like _____ apple, please.

Have _____ seat.

I'd like _____ umbrella.

25

3 Question words

Write in the question words: **Who? Whose? Where? What? Why? How? How much? How old?**

a) "_____ is that bag?"   "I think it's Sam's."

b) "_____ is Fawzia?"   "She's in the sitting room."

c) "_____ is the cake?"   "It's delicious!"

d) "_____ is your son?"   "He's six months."

e) "_____ do you like that book?"   "Because it's interesting."

f) "_____ 's your address?"   "P.O. Box 432, Jubail, Saudi Arabia."

g) "_____ is that car?"   "Five thousand dollars."

h) "_____ is that?"   "That's my uncle, Abdul Rahman."

Look!

have and have got

I **have** two children.
I **have got** two children.

I **don't have** any children.
I **haven't got** any children.

Do you have any children?
Have you got any children?

---

4 Write

> *The Present Simple Tense*
>
> I like ...
> I don't like ...   Yes, I do.
> Do you like ... ?   No, I don't.

Make sentences with **don't**. For example:

    I like Cairo in the winter. (summer)
    I don't like Cairo in the summer.

a) I speak French very well. (English)

---

b)   I like my house very much. (my job)

_____

c)   I know their daughter's name. (their son's name)

_____

d)   I have three brothers. (any sisters).

_____

Make questions with **Do you...?** For example:

    like/music?   Do you like music?

e)   like/your job?   _____

f)   speak/Arabic?   _____

g)   know/my village?   _____

h)   have/a car?   _____

5   Ask and answer

Dates.

23/5/95 = 23rd May 1995

What's the date?

It's the twenty-third of May nineteen ninety-five

Ask your partner: **What's the date? It's the ...**

a)   2nd Jan. 1996   f)   11th Apr. '87
b)   25/9/85   g)   23/6/97
c)   31st Oct. '99   h)   1/12/87
d)   3/12/94   i)   17th Sept. 2002
e)   14th Aug. 2001   j)   22/5/99

What's today's date? It's the _____

_____

6 Months of the year

What are these months?

a) __ __ l y

b) D__ c__ __ b__ __

c) M __ r c__

d) S__ p t__ m __ __ r

e) __ p r__ __

f) __ a __

g) J __ __ e

h) __ a n__ __ r y

i) __ o v__ __ __ e r

j) F__ __ r u__ __ y

k) __ __ t __ b__ __

l) A__ g __ __ __

Now write them in order.

January _____

7 In the office

Match the words with the pictures: **filing cabinet, shelves, typewriter, stamp, envelope, address, computer**

8 Food and drink

Find six things to eat and six things to drink.

```
X  R  T  E  A  J  L  S
B  R  J  U  I  C  E  A
I  Z  H  F  Y  B  M  L
S  T  R  O  M  R  O  A
C  H  I  C  K  E  N  D
U  B  C  F  Q  A  A  X
I  M  E  A  T  D  D  O
T  I  V  W  A  T  E  R
Q  L  G  P  I  C  H  E
A  K  C  O  F  F  E  E
```

9 Write

VERB   +   -ING

cook   -ing   = cooking
read   -ing   = reading

Write sentences about the pictures.

For example:

I like cooking.

I don't like reading.

I like cooking   I don't like reading

a) _____

b) _____

c) _____

d) _____

PUNCTUATION

10 Write

Put in the punctuation and the capital letters.

a)   would you like some more salad   _____

b)   whats your date of birth   _____

c)   i was born in baghdad in iraq   _____

d)   have you got a driving licence   _____

e)   i dont like learning english   _____

f)   mr   m h   ali   _____

     p o box 234   _____

     damascus   _____

     syria   _____

SPELLING

11 Look

Find *two* mistakes in each line.

a) cooking, driveing, playing, reading, waching
b) bread, cake, meat, slad, sandewich, rice
c) permit, dibloma, pass, document, certificat
d) streat, district, city, country, campany, name
e) guest, gard, garage, goal, galass, green
f) STOP, DANGRE, VISITORS, NO SMOKKING, SLOW, NO PARKING

PRONUNCIATION

12 Match

Match the words that have the same sounds.

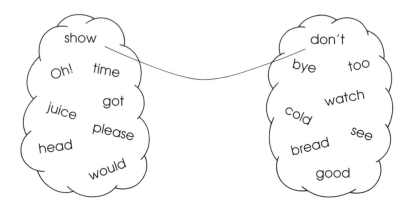

READ AND WRITE

13 Read

Read about these people:

My name's Nadia. I'm a teacher and I'm from Beirut in Lebanon. I'm married and I have two children. I like playing sports, but I don't like swimming. I also like learning languages and at the weekend I like visiting my friends and relatives in Beirut. I have a car, but I don't like driving. The roads are very busy!

I'm Gamal. I'm from Alexandria in Egypt. I'm a taxi driver and I like driving. In the evening I like watching television or reading a book. I don't like playing sports, but I like watching them on television. I have a wife and six children. I speak some English, but I don't like learning languages. I'm not a good student.

My name is Waleed. I am an engineer in a big oil company in Yemen. I am single. I like playing sports very much and I also like fishing and swimming. I don't like reading and I don't like watching television, because I think they are boring. I don't like visiting relatives, because I don't have enough time. I have a very busy life.

I'm Suhair and I come from Sharjah in the United Arab Emirates. I'm a secretary in a small insurance company. I'm married, but I don't have any children. I like shopping, reading and learning languages. I speak English and Farsi quite well and I understand a little Urdu. I don't like watching television very much in the evening. I like visiting my sisters and my parents.

Who are they? Write the names: **Nadia, Gamal, Waleed, Suhair**

NAME	visiting relatives	driving	playing sports	watching TV	reading	learning languages
a) _____	✗		✓	✗	✗	
b) _____	✓			✗	✓	✓
c) _____		✓	✗	✓	✓	✓
d) _____	✓	✗	✓			

14 Match

Match the questions with the answers to make a dialogue.

a) Some more juice?
b) Here you are.
c) Would you like a cold drink?
d) No, I haven't. But I've got some orange juice.
e) Have some dates.

A: _____

B: Yes, I would. Have you got any lemonade?

A: _____

B: Orange juice is fine.

A: _____

B: Thank you.

A: _____

B: Yes, please. Hmmm. They're very sweet.

A: _____

B: No thanks. That's enough.

15 Write

Read about Nadia, Gamal, Waleed, and Suhair again. Now write a paragraph about your life. What's your name? Where are you from? What's your job? What do you like doing?

STORY: HELLO LONDON 4

UNIT 3 MY LIFE

Lesson 1   I live in Doha

1   Listen and read

My name's Jameel Salah. I'm Qatari. I was born in Doha in 1965. I live in a district of Doha called Daphne. My apartment is near the sea. I live with my wife, my two sons and my wife's mother. I'm an accountant and I work for a small company in Doha. The name of the company is ARK Limited. In the evenings I study English at the Gulf Language School. I like learning English, but I don't have a lot of free time.

I'm Khadija Saeed. I'm from Cairo and I'm Egyptian. I was born in 1975. I was born in a suburb of Cairo called Heliopolis, but I don't live there now. I live in Zamalik with my parents and my three sisters. We have a small flat near the River Nile. a secretary and I work for a company called Egypt Tours. In my free time I like playing tennis and learning about Egyptian history.

2   Write

Name: Jameel Salah	
Born: _____	Year: _____
Live: _____	
Job: _____	
Company: _____	

Name: _____	
Born: _____	Year: _____
Live: _____	
Job: _____	
Company: _____	

33

Look!

do and *don't*

I		live ...
You		work ...
We		have ...
		like ...

I	**don't**	live ...
You		work ...
We		have ...
		like ...

Do	I	live ... ?
	you	work ... ?
	we	have ... ?
		like ... ?

Where **do** you live?   I live in ...

3   Listen and say

Where do you live?

Do you live in London?

4   Ask and answer

Ask five people.

A Where do you live?	**B** I live in...
NAME	DISTRICT/CITY
1. _____	_____
2. _____	_____
3. _____	_____
4. _____	_____
5. _____	_____

> **Look!**
>
> The verbs: *have* and *have got*
>
> | *have* | *have got* |
> |---|---|
> | I **have** two children. | I **have got** two children. |
> | I don't **hav**e much time. | I **haven't got** much time. |
> | Do you **hav**e a car? | **Have you got** a car? |

5 Match

Match the sentences with the pictures.

a) I live in a small house.
b) I work in an office.
c) I don't have much time.
d) I like playing tennis.

6 Write

Write in these words: **in, live, do, flat, have, don't**

A: Where (a) _____ you live, Khadija?

K: In Cairo.

A: Do you (b) _____ in the centre?

K: Yes. I live (c) _____ Zamalik.

A: Do you (d) _____ a house?

K: No, we (e) _____. We have a small (f) _____.

Write in these words: **don't, have, am, do, like, are**

B: (g) _____ you from Saudi Arabia, Jameel?

J: No, I'm not. I (h) _____ from Qatar.

B: (i) _____ you live in Doha?

J: Yes, I do. We (j) _____ an apartment near the sea.

B: Do you (k) _____ living in an apartment?

J: No, I (l) _____. It's very small.

7 Listen

Put these in the right lists.

secretary, apartment, lemonade, interesting, delicious, Pakistan, cigarette, September, diploma, difficult, engineer, company, accountant, date of birth, relatives

□ ■ □
secretary

_____
_____
_____
_____

□ ■ ■
apartment

_____
_____
_____
_____

□ □ ■
lemonade

_____
_____
_____
_____

Lesson 2	Where do you work?

1 Listen and write

Write **A, B, C** or **D**.

A

Which country are you from?
We're from Thailand.
And where do you work?
Here in Muscat. We work for LBC Motors. We're mechanics.

B

What's your job, Peter?
I'm a teacher.
Which subject do you teach?
English. I work for Capital English School.

C

Do you work in Riyadh?
No, I don't. I work in Dhahran in a hospital.
Which hospital?
The Awal Hospital.
And what do you do?
I'm a doctor.

D

Where do you work, Adel?
Here. At the airport.
Are you a steward?
No. I work in an office. I'm an accountant.

2   What are their jobs?

a)   Peter is _____ _____

b)   The two men from Thailand are _____.

c)   The woman is _____ _____.

d)   Adel is _____ _____.

Look!

Where do you work?

	an office.
in	a factory.
	Dubai.
	ABC Limited.
for	an engineering company.
	my uncle.
at	the airport.

3 Match

Match the job with the company/place.

a) bus driver
b) steward (stewardess)
c) mechanic
d) teacher
e) businessman (woman)
f) cashier

MANAMA GIRLS SECONDARY SCHOOL

Awal Trading Company

4 Ask and answer

Choose a job from the list above. Now ask and answer.

A	B
Where do you work?	I work at ... I work for ... I work in ...

A	B
What do you do? What's your job?	I'm a ...

Look!

Which?
A: Where do you work?
B: In a hospital.
A: **Which** hospital?
B: The Awal Hospital.

Which subject do you teach?
Which company do you work for?

5 Listen and say

Sounds and spelling. Listen.

b**u**siness, b**u**sinessman   a w**o**man, two w**o**men

Say these words. They all have the "**i**" sound.

b**u**siness, w**o**men, wh**i**ch, w**i**th, s**i**t, **i**n, **E**nglish

6 Listen and say

Say the "**er**" sound. The "**r**" is silent!

work, word, her, third, nurse, learn, first, shirt, earth, German, Germany

A: I'm a nurse.
B: A nurse? Where do you work?
A: I work in Germany.
B: In Germany? Are you German?
A: Yes, I'm a German nurse!

"Which car would you like, my son?"

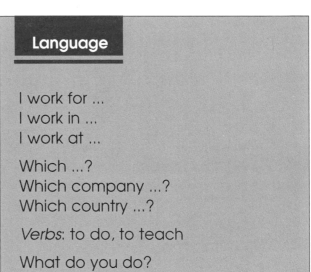

Language

I work for ...
I work in ...
I work at ...

Which ...?
Which company ...?
Which country ...?

Verbs: to do, to teach

What do you do?

Lesson 3 My children go to school

1 Listen

Sarah is with Latifa's cousin, Habiba. It is Thursday morning and they are in the park with Habiba's children.

Sarah: How old are your children, Habiba?
Habiba: Well, Bashir is seven and Waleed is eight - and little Amna here is eighteen months.

Sarah:	Which one is Bashir?
Habiba:	That's Bashir - there. The one with brown hair.
Sarah:	Oh I see - on the swing. Do the boys go to school?
Habiba:	Yes. They both go.
Sarah:	Do they like it?
Habiba:	Yes, they do. They love it. They're very happy there.
Sarah:	Really? Which school do they go to?
Habiba:	Hamad Town Primary School.
Sarah:	What's it like? Is it new?
Habiba:	Yes, it's new and it's quite big. I think it's very good.

Put a tick (✓) or a cross (✗)

a) Habiba has two children.   (   )
b) Bashir is on the swing.   (   )
c) Bashir and Waleed go to a primary school.   (   )
d) They don't like school very much.   (   )
e) The school is a new school.   (   )

Look!

primary school   intermediate school   secondary school

Look!

do and *don't*

They go to school.
They **don't** go to school.

Do they go to school?   Yes, they **do**.
                               No, they **don't**.

2   Match

Match these verbs with the pictures: **love, hate, like, don't like**

3   Look and say

love ...
I like ...
don't like ...
hate ...

For example: I don't like ice-cream.
                     I hate driving.

4   Write

Write in these words: **hate, go, they, don't**

A: Do your children (a) _____ to school?

B: Yes, (b) _____ do, but they (c) _____ like it.

A: No? Why not?

B: Because they are lazy! They (d) _____ studying.

Write in these words: **but, to, secondary, subjects, love, which**

C: (e) _____ school do you go (f) _____, girls?

D: Zarqa Girls (g) _____ School.

C: And which (h) _____ do you like?

E: I like mathematics and Arabic, (i) _____ I don't like science. It's boring.

C: And you, Lulwa?

D: I like geography and I (j) _____ history. I think it's great!

5 Listen and say

These words all have the "A" sound:

gate, late, hate, wait, lazy, play, eight, grey, say, name, baby, date, radio, snake

Now say these words with the "e" sound:

get, let, secondary, centre, secretary, subject, mechanic, tennis, relative, cigarette

6 Listen and tick

a) ☐ get   ☐ gate

b) ☐ get   ☐ gate

c) ☐ get   ☐ gate

d) ☐ get   ☐ gate

e) ☐ let   ☐ late

f) ☐ let   ☐ late

g) ☐ let   ☐ late

h) ☐ let   ☐ late

Language

Present Simple Tense: they
which one?

Verbs: to go, to hate, to love

1 Read

2 Match

Match these verbs with the pictures: **show, give, open, close**

Look!

Open	the book.	
Close	the window.	
Show	me	your homework.
Give	him	the book.
	her	
	Mohsin	

3 Match

Match these words with the pictures: **pen, keys, watch, book, money, paper, photograph**

4 Look and say

Ask your partners.

Give	me	the watch.
Show	him	money.
	her	etc.
	Mohsin	
	Nora	

"Show Nora the photograph."

Look!

Give Nora the pen.
Give **her** the pen.
Give the pen to **her**.

---

5 Write

Write: **me, her** or **him**

a) That's my pen! Give it to _____.

b) Khalid's hungry. Give _____ some sandwiches.

c) There's a guard at the gate. Show _____ your permit.

d) Mrs Brown isn't very well. Give _____ some water.

e) Who are you? Show _____ your identification card.

f) I think that's Lulwa's handbag. Give it to _____.

6 Listen and say

Sounds and spelling

photograph, **f**ull, enou**gh**

7 Listen and tick

Tick (✓) the sentence you hear.

a) Where's my cap? ☐
   Where's my cab? ☐

b) What a beautiful peach! ☐
   What a beautiful beach! ☐

c) Be careful! There's a pea on your chair. ☐
   Be careful! There's a bee on your chair. ☐

d) Where's my pen? ☐
   Where's my Ben? ☐

e) It's pouring! ☐
   It's boring! ☐

Look!

> Give me some milk.

> Can I have some milk?

Language

Object pronouns: me, him, her

Verbs: to give, to open, to close

Give me
Show him
      her

Be quiet!

STUDY

Present Simple Tense - verb: to live

I	live		I	don't live		Do I	live	...?
You	live		You	don't live		Do you	live	...?
We	live		We	don't live		Do we	live	...?
They	live		They	don't live		Do they	live	...?

Where do you live?
Do you live in Beirut?   Yes, I do.
                           No, I don't.

Which?

Which car would you like?
Which school do you go to?
Which country are you from?

Which one is Bashir?

Object pronouns: me, you, him, her

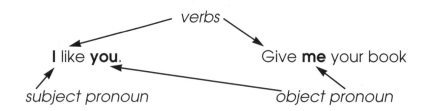

Subject	Object
I	me
you	you
he	him
she	her

---

a lot of

I don't have much time.
I don't have many friends.

I don't have **a lot of** time.
I don't have **a lot of** friends.

NEW WORDS

Learn these words:

Verbs	*Jobs*	*Other*	*Animals*
to live	accountant	factory	elephant
to work	businessman	watch	monkey
to play	cashier	photograph	fish
to learn	steward	paper	camel
to go	stewardess	company	snake
to love		apartment	
to hate		tennis	
to open		page	
to close		sea	
to give		flat	
		window	
		homework	
Adjectives	*Subjects*	Middle East	
quiet	history	trading	
noisy	mathematics	transport	
boring	geography	motor	
lazy	science		
	Arabic		
	Schools		
	primary		
	intermediate		
	secondary		

_____   _____

_____   _____

_____   _____

_____   _____

_____   _____

_____   _____

_____   _____

_____   _____

UNIT 4 FAMILY AND FRIENDS

Lesson 1 **My brother lives in Beirut**

1 Listen and read

This is my brother, Hamid. He was born in Kuwait, but he lives in Beirut. He's a student at the American University of Beirut. He studies Medicine.

And this is a photo of my grandfather, Saeed. He's a trader in the market. He's very clever. He speaks four languages - Arabic, English, Farsi and Urdu. He also speaks a little French.

This is my younger sister Warqa. I like her very much. She's very sweet and kind. She's only sixteen, so she's still at school. She goes to secondary school.

And this is my older brother, Abdul Karim. He's very nice, too. He's a security guard and he works in a bank. He likes fishing in his free time. Sometimes he catches a fish!

2 Write

Write the names.

a) Who likes fishing?   _____

b) Who studies medicine?   _____

c) Who speaks four languages?   _____

d) Who still goes to school?   _____

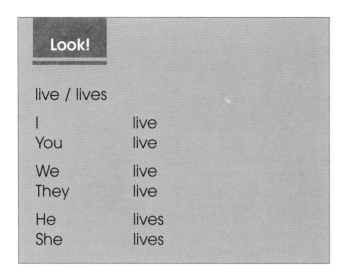

Look!

live / lives

I	live
You	live
We	live
They	live
He	lives
She	lives

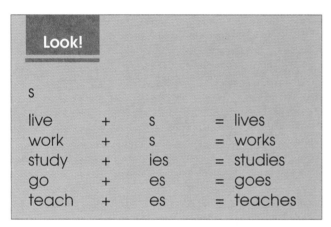

Look!

s

live	+	s	= lives
work	+	s	= works
study	+	ies	= studies
go	+	es	= goes
teach	+	es	= teaches

3 Write

Write in these verbs: **likes, speaks, goes, lives, studies, works**

a) Hamad _____ in a house near the market.
b) My cousin _____ for a big bank.
c) Nadia _____ playing the piano.
d) My friend_____English very well.
e) Hassan _____ History at Cairo University.
f) My daughter, Jamila, _____ to primary school.

4 Listen and say

These verbs end in the "**sss**" sound: **likes, works, hates, speaks**

These verbs end in the "**zzz**" sound: **lives, loves, studies, plays, goes, has**

These verbs end in the "**iz**" sound: **teaches, watches, catches**

49

5 Look and say

Use the verbs: **lives, works** (**for/in**).

Example: "Sam lives in Dallas. He works for an American oil company."

Sam (Dallas – an oil company)

Tom (Amman – the Habib Bank)

Hassan (Aswan – an hotel)

Gary (Dhahran – ARAMCO).

Mary (Amman – an office)

Sarah (Muscat – a hospital),

Latifa (Sur – a secondary school)

John (London – ABC Limited),

Peter (Bahrain – Capital English School)

Mohammad (Dammam – a ministry)

6 Write

Put these words in order to make sentences.

a)   is/ good/ Peter Parker/ a / very/ teacher
b)   well/ Najwa/ very/ I think/ sings
c)   sister/ English/ well/ quite/ speaks/ my
d)   good/ a/ isn't Ahmed/ driver/ very
e)   teaches/ very/ Peter/ English/ well

Look!

good/well

She's a very **good** singer.
She sings very **well**.

He's a **good** football player.
He plays football very **well**.

Look!

was born

He **was born** in Kuwait.

I	was	born
You	were	born
He	**was**	born
She	**was**	born

Language

Present Simple Tense: he, she

go/well
he/she was born

Verbs: to teach, to watch, to catch, to speak

50

1   Listen and read

Latifa is at a friend's wedding party. Sarah is her guest.

Latifa: Would you like some more juice, Sarah?

Sarah: Yes, please. Who's that woman, Latifa?

Latifa: Which one?

Sarah: The one in the red dress.

Latifa: Oh, that's Kamila. She's my cousin.

Sarah: Does she live here in Sur?

Latifa: No. She doesn't live in Oman. She lives in Saudi Arabia. In Jeddah.

Sarah: Why's that?

Latifa: Well, her husband is from Jeddah.

Sarah: I see. She's very pretty.

Latifa: Yes, she is. She's clever too. She's a lecturer.

Sarah: Where does she work?

Latifa: At King Abdul Aziz University in Jeddah.

Sarah: And which subject does she teach?

Latifa: I'm not sure. Come on. Let's ask her!

Put a tick (✓), a cross (✗) or D (for "don't know").

a)   Kamila is Latifa's cousin.

b)   Kamila lives in Sur in Oman.

c)   Kamila's husband is from Saudi Arabia.

d)   Kamila is a university lecturer.

e)   She teaches mathematics.

does		*do/does*					
Kamila lives in Jeddah.		I			I		
Does she live in Oman?		You	don't live ... Do		you	live...?	
She **doesn't** live in Oman.		We			we		
(She **does** not live in Oman.)		They			they		
		He	doesn't live Does		he	live ...?	
		She			she		

2 Write

These sentences are not true. Write them out with **doesn't**.

Example: Sarah likes cooking. Sarah **doesn't like** cooking.

a) Kamila lives in Muscat. _____

b) Kamila works in a hospital. _____

c) Latifa teaches in a university. _____

d) Sarah speaks Arabic very well. _____

e) Latifa knows her cousin very well. _____

3 Read

Read more about Kamila.

Kamila is married to Jaber and they live in Jeddah in Saudi Arabia. She is a lecturer at the university and she teaches science. They have three children, two girls and a boy. She speaks three languages - Arabic, English and French. She also speaks a little Turkish.

4 Ask and answer

Ask questions with *does* about Kamila.

	A			**B**
Does	Kamila	live	...?	Yes, she does.
		work		no, she doesn't.
		teach		
		speak		
		have		

Example: Does Kamila live in Oman? No, she doesn't.

Now ask questions with **is**.

	A	B
Is she	married?	Yes, she is.
	a doctor?	No, she isn't.
	clever?	
	from Saudi Arabia?	
	Latifa's sister?	

5 Match

Match these words with the pictures of the **clothes**:

a red dress	a blue jacket	a brown skirt
gold shoes	a green and yellow shirt	grey trousers
a red cap	a white T-shirt	a black suit

6 Ask and answer

A: Who's that man?
B: Which one?
A: The one in the red cap.
B: That's Mike.

Language

Present Simple Tense: does/doesn't
the one ...
also/too/both

Vocabulary: clothes, colours

1   Listen and write A, B, C or D

A
How much is that jacket, please?
Sixty dinars
Sixty or sixteen?
Sixty - of course!
Oh that's too much.

B
I'd like that dress.
The blue and yellow one?
No. The green and pink one. Is it expensive?
No. It only costs forty pounds.
I'll have it.

C
How much is that car?
Which one?
The blue and silver sports car.
Ah yes. It's a beautiful car and it's not very old.
Yes, but how much does it cost?
Five thousand five hundred dinars. It's a bargain!

D
I'd like some white shirts.
How many?
Three, I think. How much are they?
Ten riyals each.
OK. I'll have three.

2   Write

a)   The jacket costs _____

b)   The dress costs _____

c)   The shirts cost _____ each.

d)   The sports car costs _____

> **Look!**
>
> *it*
>
> How much **does** it cost?
> **It** costs ...

3 Listen and say

How much is that car?

How much does it cost?

4 Listen and say

Numbers: 1,000 - 10,000

1,000 - **a thousand**, 2,000 - **two thousand**, 2,500 - **two thousand five hundred**,
5,300 - **five thousand, three hundred**, 9,800 - **nine thousand, eight hundred**

> **Look!**
>
> 3,450 = three thousand, four hundred
> and fifty

5 Ask and answer

A		B
How much is the ...?	...	riyals
How much does the ... cost?		dinars
		dirhams
		pounds
		dollars

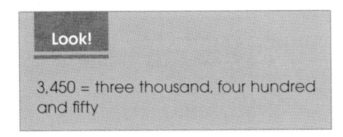

Price list	**Price list**
dress - 1,500 riyals	dress
car	car - 6,700 dinars
cap - 240 dirhams	cap
suit - 3,300 pounds	suit
shirt	shirt - 480 dirhams
picture	picture - 1,200 riyals
watch - 8,900 dinars	watch
jacket	jacket - 2,500 pounds

6 Act it out!

A   You want to buy a camera. You have only 5,000 dirhams.
B   You have a camera. The price is 6,000 dirhams.

A   You have a Datsun car. The price is 2,500 dinars.
B   You want to buy a Datsun car. You have only 2,200 dinars.

Use these words:

How much is ...? How much does ... cost?
That's too much! It's a bargain.   That's cheap/expensive.
It's very good/old ... Last price!

7 Listen and say

These words have the letter "r".

price, trousers, grey, dress, green, primary, street, brother

The "r" is silent in these words:

sports car, far, party, arm, Mars, car park, bargain

> **Language**
>
> *Present Simple Tense:* it
>
> It costs ...
> How much does it cost?
>
> *Numbers:* 1,000 - 10,000
>
> *Verb:* to cost

Lesson 4   **Congratulations!**

1 Read and match

a)   Congratulations!
b)   This is my brother-in-law, Mustapha. He comes from Aswan.
c)   Mustapha has a new baby daughter.
d)   Pleased to meet you. How do you do?

2 Listen and say

☐ ☐ ☐ ☐ ☐
congratulations

☐ ☐ ☐ ☐
brother-in-law

3 Look and say

A	**B**
I've got a new job!	Well done!
I've got my driving licence.	That's excellent!
	great!
	very good!
	fantastic!
	Congratulations!

It's my birthday today.	Happy Birthday!

Look!

brother-in-law	mother-in-law	son-in-law
sister-in-law	father-in-law	daughter-in-law

4 Match

Match these relatives:

cousin, grandfather, son-in-law, grandson, daughter-in-law, uncle, brother-in-law, sister

a) your son's wife
b) your father's son
c) your daughter's son
d) your husband's brother

e) your mother's father
f) your aunt's daughter
g) your daughter's husband
h) your brother's sister

Look!

Verb: to come from

Where are you from?	I'm from Saudi Arabia.
Where **do** you **come** from?	I **come** from Saudi Arabia.

5 Write

Write in these words: **do, well done, meet, come, got, sister-in-law**

A: This is my (a) _____, Salwa.

B: How (b)_____ you do?

C: Pleased to (c)_____ you.

B: Where do you (d)_____ from, Salwa?

C: From Syria.

A: Salwa (e)_____ a new job today.

B: Really? (f)_____

Write in these words: **wife, congratulations, have, boy, birthday**

A: (g)_____ a piece of cake, Peter.

B: Thanks. Is it your (h)_____?

A: No. My (i)_____ and I have a new baby.

B: (j)_____. A boy or a girl?

A: A (k)_____. His name's Omar.

6 Listen

Say these long words. Where is the "stress". Put a cross.(x)

O   O O O O   O O O O O   O O O   O   O O   O O   O   O O
congratulations   university   primary school   intermediate   secondary

O O O O   O   O O   O O O O   O O O O O
engineering   mathematics   Happy Birthday   Middle East Airlines

I've got a new job.

Well done! Is it a good position?

Yes. It's a very high position

Language

congratulations, well done, excellent, great, fantastic, Happy Birthday

Relatives: ... -in-law

Verb: to come from

STUDY

Present Simple Tense - verb: to live

He	lives	He	doesn't live	Does he	live ...?
She	lives	She	doesn't live	Does she	live ....?
It	lives	It	doesn't live	Does it	live ...?

Where does he live?
Does he live in Beirut?   Yes, he does.
                                 No, he doesn't.

---

was/were

I	was	born
You	were	born
He	was	born
She	was	born

Where was he born?
Where was she born?

---

good/well

He's a **good** football player.
He plays football **well**.

---

too/also/both

Ann Barry likes cooking and writing letters.

She likes learning English **too**.
She **also** likes learning English.

Hassan and his brother **both** work in a restaurant.
They are **both** waiters.

The one ...

Who's that funny man?
Which man?
The one in the black cap.

Who's that woman?
Which woman?
The one in the red dress.

NEW WORDS

Learn these words:

Colours	*Clothes*
pink	trousers
silver	shirt
gold	skirt
	suit
	shoes
	dress

Adjectives	*Other*
clever	great
kind	fantastic
nice	excellent
funny	well done
younger	congratulations
older	sweet
pretty	It's a bargain.
	It's too much.
	Last price!

Verbs
to teach
to watch
to catch
to cost
to come from

Relatives	*Animals*
brother-in-law	horse
sister-in-law	dog
father-in-law	cat
mother-in-law	
son-in-law	*jobs*
daughter-in-law	trader
	security guard
	lecturer
	singer

Other
wedding
party
price
sports car

_____   _____

_____   _____

_____   _____

_____   _____

_____   _____

_____   _____

_____   _____

REVIEW UNIT B

GRAMMAR

The Present Simple Tense: **to be**

I	am	I	am not	Am I ...?
You	are	You	are not	Are you ...?
He	is	He	is not	Is he ...?
She	is	She	is not	Is she ...?
It	is	It	is not	Is it ...?
We	are	We	are not	Are we ...?
They	are	They	are not	Are they ...?

---

1   Write

Write: **am ('m), are ('re), is ('s), am not ('m not), are not (aren't)** or **is not (isn't)** in the spaces.

a)   "Where _____ you from?" "I _____ from Baghdad."

b)   _____ "Salem and Bashir your relatives?"

     "No, they _____. They _____ friends."

c)   "_____ Sudan quite small?"

     "No, they _____. It _____ very big."

d)   "_____ you a visitor?" "No, I _____. I work here."

e)   "_____ your sister a doctor?" "Yes, she _____."

f)   "What _____ the school like?" "It _____ new."

g)   "You _____ late!" "Yes. I _____ sorry."

h)   "_____ you hungry?" "No, we _____."

The Present Simple Tense: **to live**

I	live	I	don't live	Do	I	live ...?
You		You			you	
We		We			we	
They		They			they	

He	lives	He	doesn't live	Does	he	live ...?
She		She			she	
It		It			it	

---

2 Write

Put the verbs in the Present Simple form.

My name (a) _____ (be) Ali Abdulla. I (b) _____ (live) in a small village in Oman. It (c) _____ (be) about 50 kilometres from Muscat. I (d) _____ (be) a farmer, but I (e) _____ (not work) very much now. I (f) _____ (be) quite old! I (g) _____ (have) five children and three grandchildren. My son, Omar, (h) _____ (be) a clerk. He (i) _____ (work) in the Ministry of Education. My other son, Rashid, (j) _____ (not work). He (k) _____ (go) to Ruwi Secondary School. Omar and Rashid both (l) _____ (live) with my brother in Muscat. My daughter, Fatin, (m) _____ (study) Arabic at the university. She still (n) _____ (live) here with me in the village. My other daughters (o) _____ (be) married. They (p) _____ (live) in another village not far from here. Najwa (q) _____ (have) three beautiful children.

3 Write

Write **don't** or **doesn't** in these sentences.

a) I'm sorry. I _____ speak English very well.

b) My brother _____ catch many fish.

c) We _____ live in Heliopolis now. We live in Zamalik.

d) Mustapha _____ work in the kitchen. He's a waiter.

e) This sports car _____ cost very much. It's a bargain!

e) My children _____ go to school. They are too young.

g) Simon Star is very busy. He _____ have time for hobbies.

h) No. I _____ teach Arabic. I study Arabic.

i) Fatima _____ like her new office very much. It's too small.

j) Hassan's brother-in-law _____ come from Cairo. He is from Aswan.

k) Tom and Mary _____ watch television in the evening. They read.

l) My sister and I _____ study history. We study mathematics and science.

4 Write

Simon Star is in a television studio in Cairo. Write *do* or *does* in this dialogue.

Aida: Welcome to Cairo, Mr Star.

Simon: Thank you. Call me Simon, please.

Aida: All right, Simon. (a) _____ you like our city?

Simon: (b) _____ I like it? I love it. I think it's great.

Aida: I know you are from America. But which city (c) _____ you come from?

Simon: I was born in New York. But I live in Los Angeles now.

Aida: And where (d) _____ your wife come from?

Simon: She's from Miami.

Aida: What (e) _____ she do?

Simon: She's an actress. She's with me in Cairo now

Aida: (f) _____ she like visiting different countries?

Simon: She loves it. She likes going to markets.

Aida: How many children (g) _____ you have?

Simon: We have two - John and Betty. They're here in Cairo too.

Aida: (h) _____ your children like watching basketball?

Simon: John likes basketball, but Betty thinks it's boring.

Aida: (i) _____ they go to basketball games?

Simon: Sometimes, yes.

Aida: Finally, Mr St.. I mean, Simon. What (j) _____ you do in your free time?

Simon: What (k) _____ I do? Nothing. Just swimming and resting!

5 Write

Put in the pronouns: **I, you, he, she, me, you, him,** or **her.**

_ _ _ _ like _ _ _ _ _. Do _ _ _ _ like _ _ _ _ ?

Pronouns	
Subject	*Object*
I	me
you	you
he	him
she	her

Show _ _ _ _ _ our passports, Mary. _ _ _ _ _ is the immigration officer.

Give _ _ _ _ _ your seat. _ _ _ _ _ is tired.

NEW WORDS

6 Verbs

Match the verbs with the pictures.

live, open, work, study, play, catch, go, love, hate, teach, watch, close, cost.

a) _____ b) _____ c) _____ d) _____ e) _____ f) _____

g) _____ h) _____ i) _____ j) _____ k) _____ l) _____ l) _____

7 Animals

Find nine animals in the square.

```
R  P  M  V  I  K  F  C
C  H  O  R  S  E  I  A
A  G  N  E  B  S  S  T
M  Z  K  O  E  N  H  X
E  L  E  P  H  A  N  T
L  B  Y  G  U  K  I  J
A  D  T  I  G  E  R  M
C  F  U  D  O  G  Z  C
```

8 Clothes

Match the words with the pictures: **trousers, shirt, skirt, suit, shoes, dress, hat, cap, overalls, uniform**

a) ____   b) ____   c) ____   d) ____   e) ____   f) ____   g) ____   h) ____   i) ____   j) ____

9 Write

Write these words in the sentences: **price, apartment, company, secondary, wedding, photograph, watch, steward.**

a) "What's the time?" "Sorry. I haven't got a _____."

b) This is a _____ of my baby daughter, Amina.

c) Ali is a businessman. He works for his uncle's _____.

d) Hamid has got a job with Gulf Air. He's a _____.

e) Give me 1,000 dinars for the car. That's my last _____!

f) There is a big _____ party at the Good Luck Hotel.

g) We live in a small _____ near the city centre.

h) Badria teaches in a _____ school in Kuwait.

PUNCTUATION

10 Write out the paragraph with correct punctuation

my names hamid and im twenty-three years old im from damascus and im a student at in damascus university i study science and mathematics i study english too but i dont speak it very well my wifes name is sahira she doesnt come from syria shes lebanese shes also a student and she studies arabic and history we dont have any children we live with my parents in a district of damascus called al mazah in my free time i like playing basketball

_____

_____

_____

_____

_____

_____

SPELLING

11 Look

There are two spelling mistakes in every line.

a) lives, teaches, studyes, loves, costes, works, has, plays
b) who, where, whach, why, whate, whose, how
c) kind, sweet, noisy, lasy, boring, claver, pretty
d) give, sit, opin, close, have, come, showe
e) Middel East Airlines, Awal Trading Company, Expres Transport

There are five mistakes in this dialogue.

f) This is a great partey.
   Yes, it is. Who's that funny man over thare?
   Which one?
   The very fat one in the pink and white shert.
   That's my brother-in-low!
   I'm very sarry!

PRONUNCIATION

12 Match the words that have the same sounds

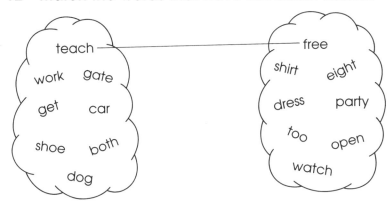

READ AND WRITE

13 Read

Read about these people.

Match the names and nationalities.

Akbar	French
Marie	Japanese
Mustapha	Indian
Yoshioa	Egyptian

A Akbar is a taxi driver. He lives in Bombay in India, but he was born in Delhi in the north. His son is a mechanic and he works in Qatar. Akbar meets many tourists. He drives them from the airport to their hotels. He doesn't speak Arabic, but he knows a few words of English. In his free time he likes reading poetry.

B Marie Dupont is an actress. She is famous for her films about the history of France. She doesn't like big cities and lives in a quiet village near Paris. She travels a lot because she makes films all over the world. At the moment she is in Lebanon.

C Mustapha Habib is a footballer. He is Egyptian, but he lives in Munich in Germany. He plays football for a club in Germany. He is a striker and scores many goals. He has a house in Munich, but he doesn't live there in the summer. He goes to Cairo in May, at the end of the football season. He is married and has three children.

D Yoshioa Masaoka is a businessman. He works for a Japanese car company. He travels to the Middle East many times every year. His company sells a lot of cars to Arab countries. Yoshioa lives in Tokyo in Japan. He likes learning languages. He speaks English and German quite well, but he doesn't speak much Arabic.

Write the correct names in the sentences: *Akbar, Marie, Mustapha, Yoshioa.*

a) _____ was born in Delhi.

b) _____ plays football in Germany.

c) _____ doesn't like big cities.

d) _____ lives in Cairo in the summer.

e) _____ is in Lebanon at the moment.

f) _____ likes reading in his free time.

g) _____ works for a car company.

h) _____ and _____ don't speak much Arabic.

14   Write about these people.

Name:	Samia Saeedi	Khalid Mohammad
Born:	Alexandria	Al Ain
Year:	1971	1969
Married/Single:	married - one daughter	single
Lives:	Cairo, Egypt	Dubai
Job:	accountant	cashier
Company:	Al Ahlia Trading	Gulf Bank
Free time/hobbies:	learning French, writing to friends,	Playing table-tennis, swimming, computers

David and his friends are visiting London Zoo.

How much is it?

Six pounds each, please.

ELEPHANTS

DO NOT FEED THE ANIMALS

SNAKES
MONKEYS TIGERS
CAMELS

Let's see the tigers now.

Help! Help! My son!

Khalid! What're you doing?

It was nothing.

Thank you very much. You were so brave.

Where do you come from?

I'm from Dubai. I'm here on holiday with my grandfather. It's our first visit to London.

And what do you do in Dubai?

I'm a student. I study Engineering at a college in Dubai.

Tell me about your grandfather. Does he come from Dubai too?

Yes he does, but he was born in Al Ain. He's a businessman and he has a small company in Dubai.

EXIT

Let's go! I don't like all these questions!

The next day.

Look at this, Khalid. You're famous!

EVENING NEWS

TOURIST HERO SAVES BOY FROM TIGER

UNIT 5 WHEN?

My day

1 Listen and read

> I work here - in the refinery. The work is quite hard and the hours are long, but the money's good. I start work early, at seven o'clock in the morning, so I usually have breakfast and lunch in the canteen. I finish work at about six in the evening and then I have dinner with my family. I sometimes work on the night shift, but I don't like that very much.

a) Where does Ahmed work?
b) When does he start work?
c) When does he finish?
d) Does he usually have breakfast at home?
e) Does he sometimes work at night?

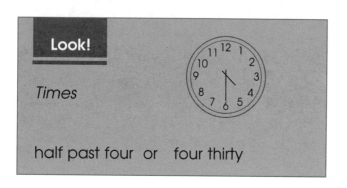

Look!

Times

half past four or four thirty

2 Match

Match these times with the clocks and watches:

six thirty, eleven o'clock, half past three, five o'clock, half past twelve, seven o'clock, one thirty, half past nine

3 Look and say

I start	work school college university	at ...
I finish at . . .		

4 Listen and say

´When do you have breakfast?

When do you have lunch?

When do you have dinner?

Look!

I have	breakfast . . . lunch dinner

5 Ask and answer

Ask three people.

A		**B**
When do you have	breakfast? lunch? dinner?	At eight o´clock. At half past one. At six thirty.

NAME	TIMES		
	breakfast	**lunch**	**dinner**
1. _____	_____	_____	_____
2. _____	_____	_____	_____
3. _____	_____	_____	_____

Look!

sometimes/usually

I (don´t)	**usually**	have breakfast in the canteen.
I	**sometimes**	work on the night shift.

6 Write

Write out these sentences with **sometimes** or **usually**.

a) Samia has breakfast with her children.   (sometimes)
b) Tom and Mary go to England in the summer.   (usually)
c) I don't watch television in the evening.   (usually)
d) My brother-in-law plays football for Al Awal club.   (sometimes)
e) We have dinner at eight o'clock.   (usually)
f) My cousin and I go shopping in the afternoon.   (sometimes)

7 Listen and say

Say the "**st**" sound.

start, stop, stairs, student, study, station, stereo, street

> ## Language
>
> When ...?
>
> sometimes/usually
>
> *Times:* half past six, six thirty
>
> *Verbs:* to start, to finish, to have

Lesson 2   What do you have for breakfast?

1 Match

Match these words with the pictures: **cheese, jam, eggs, olives, yoghurt**

2 Listen

Listen and write A, B, C or D.

A

When do you usually get up, Simon?
Late! About eight thirty or a quarter to nine.
And what do you have for breakfast?
Coffee, eggs and orange juice.

B

Do you usually get up early, Latifa?
Yes, quite early. I get up about a quarter past seven.
Do you? And what about breakfast?
I never have breakfast. Just tea.

C

What's the food like in the canteen, Ahmed?
It's not bad. I have my breakfast there.
What do you have?
Tea, bread and jam, or sometimes cheese and olives.

D

What time do you get up in the morning, Mary?
Quite early, about six fifteen. I never get up late.
And what about breakfast?
Just fruit and yoghurt usually.

What do they have for breakfast? Put a tick (✓)

	tea	coffee	bread	fruit	jam	yoghurt	eggs	orange juice	cheese	olives
Simon:	☐	☐	☐	☐	☐	☐	☐	☐	☐	☐
Latifa:	☐	☐	☐	☐	☐	☐	☐	☐	☐	☐
Ahmed:	☐	☐	☐	☐	☐	☐	☐	☐	☐	☐
Mary:	☐	☐	☐	☐	☐	☐	☐	☐	☐	☐

Look!

When...? / What time...?

When **What time**	do you get up in the morning?

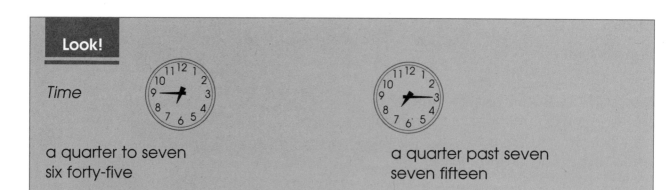

Look!

Time

a quarter to seven
six forty-five

a quarter past seven
seven fifteen

3 Look and say

What's the time?   It's ...

4 Ask and answer

Ask three people.

When do you have breakfast?   At ...
What do you (usually) have?

	NAME	TIME	BREAKFAST
1.	_____	_____	_____
2.	_____	_____	_____
3.	_____	_____	_____

Look!

never

I	usually	get up early.
	sometimes	
He/she	**never**	gets up early.

74

5 Write

Write in the words: **usually, sometimes** or **never**

a) Latifa _____ has breakfast. Just tea.

b) Ahmed _____ has breakfast in the canteen.

c) He _____ has cheese and olives for breakfast.

d) Mary _____ gets up late.

e) Ahmed _____ works at night.

f) Latifa _____ gets up at about a quarter past seven.

6 Look and say

Talk about your morning.

I	usually	get up ...
	sometimes	have ... for breakfast.
	never	start work/school ...

7 Listen and say

Say these words:

out, now, about, brown, town, house, trousers

Come on. Get up.

I hate mornings.

Why's that?
Because mornings are so early!

Language

never
just

What time ...?
a quarter to / a quarter past

Breakfast vocabulary

Verb: to get up, to pray

1 Read

Tom always gets up early and goes for a run. After that he has a shower and gets dressed. Then he has a big breakfast - eggs, toast, tea and fruit juice. At about half past seven he leaves home and drives to the bank. He usually finishes work about two thirty and then he returns home. He has lunch with his wife, Mary. In the afternoon he always rests for an hour and then he goes for a walk before dinner. In the evening Tom and Mary stay at home. Tom usually reads and then he goes to bed at about ten.

Number the pictures 1 to 8.

2 Match

Match the verbs with the pictures above.

to walk, to rest, to go (to bed), to stay, to run, to have (breakfast), to finish, to drive

Look!

to leave (home)   to return (home)

76

3 Write

Write these verbs in the text in the "**s**" form.

**to stay, to finish, to return, to walk,
to have (x2), to visit, to get up, to leave**

Latifa (a) _____ at seven fifteen. She (b) _____ just a cup of tea for breakfast. She (c) _____ home about a quarter to eight and (d) _____ to work.
At eleven o'clock she usually (e) _____ tea and a sandwich. She (f) _____
work at three o'clock and then (g) _____ home. In the evening she usually (h)
_____ at home with her family, but sometimes she
(i) _____ friends or relatives.

> **Look!**
>
> *Then ... / ... and then ...*
>
> Tom finishes work at two thirty. He drives home.
>
> Tom finishes work at two thirty **and then** he drives home.
> Tom finishes work at two thirty. **Then** he drives home.

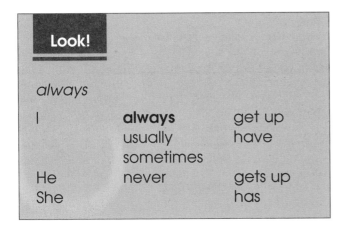

> **Look!**
>
> *always*
>
> | I | **always** | get up |
> | | usually | have |
> | | sometimes | |
> | He | never | gets up |
> | She | | has |

4 Write

Write sentences with **always, usually, sometimes** or **never**

Example: coffee / for breakfast
           I never have coffee for breakfast.

a) get up / late
b) rice / for lunch
c) stay at home / evening
d) friends / afternoon

e) tea / at night
f) go shopping / morning
g) go to bed / early

5 Look and say

a) Tell the story of Fatima's day.

b) Tell the story of Ahmed's day.

6 Listen and write

Write the verbs in the correct lists: **returns, walks, leaves, rests, visits, stays, reads, gets, drives**

"**ssss**": likes, _____

"**zzzz**": lives, _____

always

then / and then

after / before

Verbs: to get dressed, to rest, to return, to leave, to run, to read, to walk, to drive, to stay

to go to (bed)
to go for (a run)
to go for (a walk)

to have (a shower)

Lesson 4   Peter's week

1   Listen.

Peter is on a plane. He's going on holiday.

Farouq:	Where do you work?
Peter:	In Bahrain. I'm a teacher in a language school.
Farouq:	Really? I'm a teacher too. How many classes do you have?
Peter:	Four classes every day - two in the morning and two in the evening.
Farouq:	So you don't teach in the afternoons?
Peter:	No. But every Monday and Wednesday afternoon I go to my Arabic lessons.
Farouq:	Oh, you teach Arabic too?
Peter:	Oh no! I study it. I'm just a beginner.
Farouq:	And at weekends - what do you do?
Peter:	Well, on Thursday mornings I go to the supermarket and after that I have my driving lesson. Then in the afternoon I usually visit some of my friends.
Farouq:	And do you rest on Fridays?
Peter:	Not really. I always get up early and go the beach and after lunch I play tennis. And then later in the evening I prepare my classes.
Farouq:	You have a busy week!

a)   How many classes does Peter teach?
b)   Does he teach in the evenings?
c)   Does he teach Arabic?
d)   When does Peter have his Arabic classes?
e)   When does he go to the supermarket?
f)   What does he do on Friday mornings?

2 Write

Complete Peter's timetable. Write in: a) Arabic lesson, b) driving lesson, c) tennis, d) prepare classes, e) beach, f) supermarket

	SATURDAY	SUNDAY	MONDAY	TUESDAY	WEDNESDAY	THURSDAY	FRIDAY
morning	← ———— teaching ————————→						
afternoon							
evening	← ———— teaching ————————→						

Look!

on

on Monday(s)   **on** Wednesday(s)   **on** Friday(s)
                    in the morning
but: **on** Friday morning

---

3 Write

Write in these words: **prepare, later, supermarket, stay, on, afternoon**

Sam: What do you do a) _____ Thursday? _____

Ahmed: Not much. In the morning we go to the b) _____. Then we go home and c) _____ lunch.

Sam: And in the d) _____?

Fatma: We usually e) _____ at home and watch a video.

Ahmed: And we sometimes go for a walk f) _____.

Write in these words: **always, about, then, every, phone, evening, busy, after**

Sam: Are you g) _____ tomorrow morning, Salem?

Salem: Yes, I am. I go to the mosque h) _____ Friday.

Sam: And i) _____ that?

Salem: Well, I come home at j) _____ two o'clock and k) _____ we have lunch.

Sam: What about the l) _____?

Salem: I'm sorry, Sam. We m) _____ visit my wife's parents on Friday evenings.

Sam: Don't worry. I'll n) _____ again on Saturday.

4 Ask and answer

Talk to another student.

A

What do you do at the weekends?

B

On Thursday ...	I	(always)	go to ...
On Friday ...		(usually)	stay at home.
On Saturday ...		(sometimes)	visit ...
On Sunday ...			watch ...

5 Say

Tell the class about another student. What does he or she do at the weekend?

On (Thursday)	Yacoub	(always)	goes ...
		(usually)	stays ...
		(sometimes)	watches ...

> **Look!**
>
> | | *Time* |
> | I usually go to the beach | on Fridays. |
> | | in the morning. |
> | | at eight o'clock. |
>
> | *Time* | |
> | On Fridays | I usually go to the beach. |
> | In the morning | |
> | At eight o'clock | |

6 Listen and say

Say these words:

just, jacket, jeans, job, jam, orange, juice, Germany, George, engine, garage

Now say these words:

go, get, give, girl, guest, guard, big, bag, dog, glass, great, younger

7 Listen and write

Put these words in the correct lists:

weekend, get up, every, later, return, prepare, classes, because

☐ ☐
weekend

☐ ☐
get up

_____

_____

_____

_____

_____

_____

And what do you do at the weekend?

Language

on Friday
at the weekend

every

later

Verbs: to prepare, to visit

STUDY

When ...? What time ...?

When do you get up?
When do you start work?
(At) What time do you have breakfast?

---

always, usually, sometimes, never

I	**always**	get up early.
You	**usually**	go to the mosque on Fridays.
We	**sometimes**	start work at 8.
They		
He	**never**	gets up early.
She		goes to the mosque on Fridays.
		starts work at 8.

What's the time?

It's half past eight.
It's eight thirty.

It's a quarter past seven.
It's seven fifteen.

It's a quarter to four.
It's three forty-five.

---

on, in, at	every
on Friday(s)	every day / week / month / year
on Friday afternoon(s)	every Friday
in the morning / afternoon / evening	
at night	
at the weekend	

Then / and then

Tom goes for a run. He has a shower.
Tom goes for a run **and then** he has a shower.
Tom goes for a run. **Then** he has a shower.

---

after / before

I have a rest **after** lunch.
I go for a walk **before** dinner.

NEW WORDS

Learn these words:

Food	Adjectives	Verbs
yoghurt	early	to walk
cheese	hard	to leave
eggs	busy	to rest
olives		to run
jam		to go for (a run)
honey		to go for (a walk)
		to get up
		to get dressed
meals	*nouns*	to prepare
breakfast	refinery	
lunch	shower	to start
dinner	college	to stay
	weekend	to visit
	rest	to return
	night shift	to have (breakfast / a shower)
	supermarket	to pray
	class	
	lesson	
	quarter	

_____   _____

_____   _____

_____   _____

_____   _____

_____   _____

_____   _____

_____   _____

UNIT 6 ON HOLIDAY

Lesson 1   What's the weather like?

1   Match

It's ... **sunny, cloudy, windy, raining.**

2   Listen and write

Write **A, B, C** or **D**.

A

What's the weather like, Saeed?
It's hot and sunny.
Good. I'm going for a swim.
Me too.

B

Oh look!
What?
It's raining.
Raining? But it was sunny yesterday!
Well, it's raining now.

C

What's the weather like in the winter, Latifa?
Terrible! It's very cold and windy.
Does it rain?
Yes. It usually rains in January and February.

D

Are you on holiday today, Waleed?
Yes, of course. It's National Day. Everyone's on holiday.
Let's go for a picnic.
Good idea. The weather's lovely.

3 Ask and answer

A

What's the weather like?

B

It's   hot   (and ...)
cold
sunny
cloudy
windy
raining

4 Write

a) What's the weather like today?   It's _____

b) What was the weather like yesterday?   It was _____

5 Match

Match the questions with the answers.

What's Salwa like?

What's the weather like in the summer?

What's "foul medames" like?

What's your uncle like?

What's Cairo like?

What're your children like?

What's your suitcase like?

It's black with a red handle.

They're very clever.

He's tall with black hair and a moustache.

Terrible. It's very, very hot and sunny.

It's delicious.

She's short and she's got brown hair and brown eyes.

It's very big and noisy.

6 Write

Write in these words: **lovely, like, very, it's, terrible, raining**

A: What's the weather (a) _____ in Toronto, Dad?

B: (b)_____. It's (c) _____ cold and it's (d) _____.

A: Is it? It's (e) _____ here. It's sunny and (f) _____ not too hot.

B: You're lucky!

Write in these words: **weather, at, everyone, windy, quite, on**

C: How are you Sarah?

D: I'm fine thanks, Mum.

C: Are you (g) _____ work?

D: No. Today's National Day. (h) _____ is
    (i) _____ holiday.

C: Is the (j) _____ good?

D: Not bad. It's cold but (k) _____ sunny.

C: It's very (l) _____ here.

7 Listen and say

Say these words with the "**ee**" sound.

sunny, windy, cloudy, lovely, happy, thirty, very, every, early, honey, refinery, coffee

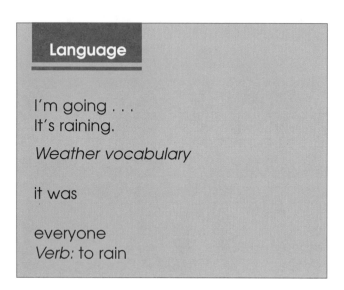

I'm going . . .
It's raining.

Weather vocabulary

it was

everyone
Verb: to rain

1   Read

It's a holiday today. Hassan and his family are going on a picnic. They are going a Adhari Park.

Now they are at Adhari Park. It is a beautiful place with many trees and a lake. There is a small cafe too. The children are playing with some toys and Hassan's wife, Nadia, is preparing the lunch. A woman is taking a photograph of her friends. Some people are walking by the lake. Hassan is sleeping under a tree.

"What are you doing Hassan?"

"I'm sleeping."

Write these words: **preparing lunch, walking, playing, sleeping**

a)   What is Hassan doing?   He's _____

b)   What is Nadia doing?   She's _____

c)   What are the children doing?   They're _____

d)   What are some people doing?   They're _____

2   Look and say

What are they doing?

He's   ...   -ing
She's   ...
They're   ...

3   Write

Write these verbs in the **-ing** form. Write them in the correct lists.

walk, prepare, swim, go, make, rain, run, play, drive, eat, take, get

A   sleeping, _____

B   sitting, _____

C   having, _____

90

4 Write

Today is a holiday. It's eleven o'clock in the morning. What is everyone doing? Put the verbs in the **-ing** form. For example:

Sam _____ some friend. (visit)

Sam **is visiting** some friends.

a) Fatima _____ lunch in the kitchen. (prepare)

b) Tom and Mary _____ to the beach. (drive)

c) Gary _____ a book in the garden. (read)

d) Ahmed and his family _____ in the park. (walk)

e) Peter _____ tennis with a friend. (play)

f) Latifa and Sarah _____ photographs. (take)

g) Saeed is in his boat. He _____. (fish)

h) Hassan _____ in the hotel. (work)

i) Jamila and Mohsin are in the sitting room. They _____ a video. (watch)

j) Mohammad _____ coffee in a cafe in the market. (have)

k) Two boys _____ in the lake. (swim)

l) Salwa _____ some coffee for her guests. (make)

Look!
What're you doing?   I'm waiting for a bus.
What're you doing?   We're waiting for a bus.

---

5 Write

What're you doing?

I _____ some fruit. (eat)

My sister and I _____ to the hospital. (go)

91

6 Listen and say

Say these words ending in "ing".

going, doing, having, walking, running, watching, sleeping, driving, making, sitting

7 Listen and say

These words have the "p" sound.

place, people, play, pray, prepare, picnic

Language

Present Continuous Tense: to be + -ing

Verbs: to take (a photograph), to wait (for), to make, to sleep, to play, to think, to learn, to look at

under a tree
by the lake

Lesson 3   In a restaurant

1 Listen and read

Tom and Mary are on holiday in Egypt. They are having dinner in a restaurant in Aswan.

Tom:	The food looks delicious.	*Waiter:*	Anything with it?
Mary:	Yes, it does. I'm quite hungry.	*Mary:*	Yes. Rice and salad.
Tom:	So am I. Ah good, the waiter's coming.	*Waiter:*	Would you like something to drink?
Waiter:	Good evening. What would you like to eat?	*Mary:*	Yes. Apple juice.
		Tom:	The same, please.
Tom:	Fish, please, with salad and potatoes.	*Waiter:*	And for dessert?
		Tom:	Chocolate ice-cream.
Waiter:	And for you, madam?	*Mary:*	Nothing for me, thanks.
Mary:	I'd like chicken.		

What are they having for dinner? Tick (v) the food and drink.

Tom			Mary	
meat	☐		meat	☐
fish	☐		fish	☐
chicken	☐		chicken	☐
beefsteak	☐		beefsteak	☐
salad	☐		salad	☐
rice	☐		rice	☐
potatoes	☐		potatoes	☐
vegetables	☐		vegetables	☐
fruit	☐		fruit	☐
yoghurt	☐		yoghurt	☐
ice-cream	☐		ice-cream	☐
apple juice	☐		apple juice	☐

2   Write

What are Tom and Mary having for dinner?

a)   Tom is having _____

b)   Mary _____

Look!

desert / dessert

☐   ☐
desert

☐   ☐
dessert

3   Listen

Listen and say these words.

☐ ☐ ☐   ☐ ☐ ☐ ☐   ☐   ☐ ☐   ☐ ☐   ☐ ☐
potatoes   vegetables   lamb kebab   beefsteak   chocolate

What would you like to eat?

What would you like to drink?

4   Act it out

A   You are the waiter. Ask:

What would you like to eat/to drink?
And for you?
Anything with it?
And for dessert?

B and **C**   You are hungry and thirsty! Choose
five things from the menu. Say:
I'd like ...

MENU

soup	vegetables
lamb kebab	potatoes
chicken	rice
fish	salad
beefsteak	bread

Dessert	*Drinks*
ice-cream	tea
fruit	coffee
cheese	Cola
chocolate cake	apple juice

> **Look!**
>
> *something/anything/nothing*
> I'd like **something** to eat. I'm hungry.
>
> Would you like **anything** with the chicken?
> No, **nothing,** thank you.

5 Write

Write in these **-ing** verbs: **looking, having, sitting, standing, coming, waiting, saying**

Miriam and her husband are (a) _____ at a table in a coffee shop. They aren't very hungry and so they are just (b) _____ sandwiches. The coffee shop is very busy. Some people are (c) _____ at the door. They are (d) _____ for a table. The waiter is very slow. Miriam is (e) _____ at her watch. "Oh, good!" she is (f) _____ to her husband. "The waiter is (g) _____ with the sandwiches."

6 Listen and write

Sounds and spelling.

Write these words in the correct lists: **steak, head, read, friend, beef, police, red, take, eight, guest, people, wait**

steak	head	read
_____	_____	_____
_____	_____	_____
_____	_____	_____

95

Waiter! There's some-thing in my soup.

It's a fly, sir.

I know it's a fly, but what is it doing in my soup?

it's swimming, sir.

> ### Language
>
> What would you like to eat/to drink?
>
> *Food vocabulary*
>
> *Verbs:* to say, to stand, to eat, to drink

Lesson 4   Where are you going?

1   Listen

A

Where are you going, Latifa?
I'm going to the supermarket.
Oh? Can I come with you?
Of course.

B

I'm sorry. I must go.
Are you going home?
No, I'm not. I'm going to the garage. It closes at six o'clock.
OK. See you later, Saeed.

C

Excuse me. Can I see your pass, please?
Sure. Here you are.
Where are you going?
To Mr Khalifa's office.
That's all right, Mr Smith. Please go in.

D

Where are you going?
The airport. We're late.
OK. Get in.
How much is it?
As you like!

Where are they going?

a) Latifa is going to _____ .

b) Ahmed _____ .

c) Sam Smith _____ .

d) The two men _____ .

Look!

Where are you going?
Are you going home?   Yes, I am.
                         No, I'm not.

---

2 Listen and say

Where are you going?

Are you going home?

3 Ask and answer

Ask four people:

Where are you going (after the lesson)?

NAME	WHERE
1 _____	_____
2 _____	_____
3 _____	_____
4 _____	_____

Look!

go in / get in

go in

get in

4 Act it out

A You are a taxi driver. Ask:

Where are you going?
OK. Get in, please.
.... dinars.

B You want a taxi to go to: the market/the airport/the bus station/the hospital

I'm going to ...
How much is it?
OK / That's too much!

Look!

must

I **must** go. I'm late.

You **must** speak to the doctor.
He **must** study every evening.

5 Numbers

Match the numbers.

ten, fifty, a hundred, five hundred, a thousand, ten thousand, a hundred thousand, five hundred thousand, a million

100,000	100	1,000,000	1,000
_____	_____	_____	_____
500,000	10	50	500
_____	_____	_____	_____
10,000			
_____			

6 Listen and say

These words all have "**th**":

thing, something, think, nothing, three thirty, anything, bath, thin

These words all have "**th**" too, but the sound is different

then, after that, with, weather, there, another, brother-in-law, the airport

A: What's that?
B: What?
A: There. There's something in the bath.
B: In the bath? There's nothing.
A: There is.
B: Oh yes. That.
A: It's thin.
B: With long legs.
A: It's horrible!

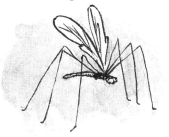

Sorry. I must go.

Language

Where are you going?

Must

Numbers: a hundred thousand, a million

Verb: to get in

The Present Continuous Tense

to be + -ing

I am	(not)	going	We are	(not)	going
You are		having	You are		having
He is		playing	They are		playing
She is		reading			reading
It is		sitting			sitting

What are you doing? I'm having lunch.
Where are you going? We're going to the market.
Are you going home? Yes, I am. / No, I'm not.

---

was / were

I was	We were
You were	You were
He was	They were
She was	
It was	

It was cold and windy yesterday.

---

must

I must go.
You must see a doctor.
He must study every evening.

---

something, anything, nothing

There's something in my soup.
Would you like anything to drink?
There's nothing in the fridge.

What would you like to eat? I'd like meat and rice.
What would you like to drink? I'd like some water.

---

under
He's sleeping under a tree.

by
They are walking by the lake.

NEW WORDS

Learn these words:

Adjectives
sunny
cloudy
windy
lovely
terrible
horrible

Food
soup
potatoes
vegetables
lamb
beef
beefsteak
kebab
chocolate

Verbs
to rain
to take (a photograph)
to wait (for)
to say
to stand
to get in
to make
to listen (to)
to sleep
to play
to think
to look at

Other
yesterday
the same
of course
see you later!
see you soon!
something
anything
nothing
everyone

Nouns
holiday
picnic
place
desert
dessert
toys
menu
lake
cafe

_____   _____

_____   _____

_____   _____

_____   _____

_____   _____

_____   _____

REVIEW UNIT C

GRAMMAR

---

always / usually / sometimes / never

I		get up early.
You	always	
We	usually	
They	sometimes	
	never	
He	gets up early.	
She		
It		

Look!

I **sometimes** visit my aunt on Thursdays.
I don't **usually** work in the evening.
Do you **always** stay at home at the weekends?

1 Write

Put the words in the right order.

a) afternoon / sometimes / in / rest / I / the
b) on / never / Sam / Fridays / works /
c) leaves / Nadia / at / thirty / office / always / two / her
d) don't / to / they / school / morning / the / walk / usually / in
e) picnic / for / in / summer / never / a / the / we / go
f) in / watch / you / always /evenings / do / television / the / ?
g) doesn't / the /Tunisia / summer / usually / it / in / rain / in
h) have / Ahmed / does / canteen / the / in / always / breakfast / ?

2 Write

Write four sentences about your life with **always, usually, sometimes** and **never**

For example: I always get up at six o'clock.

a) _____

b) _____

c) _____

d) _____

Now write four sentences about a friend or a relative.

For example: My brother never drives to work. He always walks.

e) _____

f) _____

g) _____

h) _____

The Present Continuous Tense

to be + –ing

I am	(not) watching	We are	(not)	watching
You are		You are		
He is		They are		
She is				
It is				

Look!

I am reading a letter.
I am not writing a letter.
Are you listening to me?

3 What are they doing?

What are the people in the pictures doing? Write sentences.

a) Noor   b) Salwa   c) Hanan and Ibtisam   d) Jalal and Rashid

e) Khalid   f) Ilham   g)   h)

a) _____

b) _____

c) _____

d) _____

e) _____

f) _____

g) _____

h) _____

4 On the telephone

Put the verb in the Continuous form.

Sue: Hello, Samia. This is Sue.

Samia: Hello! How are you?

Sue: Fine. What (a) _____ you _____ (do)?

Samia: I (b) _____ _____ (prepare) lunch.

Sue: Oh. (c) _____ you _____ (cook) lamb?

Samia: No. We (d) _____ _____ (not have) a big lunch. Just a snack.
          Come and have lunch with us!

Sue: No, thanks. Where are the children?

104

Samia:	Upstairs.

Sue: (e) _____ they _____ (read) their school books?

Samia: No. They (f) _____ _____ (not read). They (g) _____ _____ (listen) to music. They are very noisy!

Sue: What (h) _____ Aziz _____ (do)? Is he at work?

Samia: No. He (i) _____ _____ (not work). He's here at home. He (j) _____ _____ (watch) television, I think.

Sue: Where (k) _____ you _____ (go) after lunch, Samia?

Samia: We (l) _____ _____ (stay) at home. Why?

Sue: Well, I (m) _____ _____ (go) to the park. Would you all like to come with me?

Samia: Yes. That would be nice.

Sue: OK. See you later.

5 Write

Write **on, in** or **at**.

a) I'll see you tomorrow _____ ten o'clock.

You mean, ten o'clock _____ the morning?

No, ten o'clock _____ night.

b) When were you born, Grandmother?

I was born _____ 1910, _____ June.

c) Are you _____ holiday this week?

No. We never have our holidays _____ the winter.

d) Are you busy _____ the weekend?

I'm busy _____ Thursday. But I'm free _____ Friday afternoon.

e) Where's Saeed. Is he _____ work?

I think he's _____ home _____ the moment.

6 Question words

Match the questions with the answers.

a) When does the class start?
b) Which company do you work for?
c) Why do you always drive to my house? It's not far.
d) Who is that man?
e) Where do you come from?

f)   What's that! Under the cupboard?
g)   Whose jacket is this?
h)   How is the soup?
i)   How much is this?
j)   How many days are there in this month?

It's nothing.

Khalifa's.

Because I'm lazy!

Saeed.

Soon.

Middle East Trading.

Fantastic!

Five pounds.

I'm not sure.

Algeria.

NEW WORDS

7   Verbs

Match the verbs with the noun.

Verb
get
get in
make
mat for
listen for
go for
cook
start
return

North
tea
work
the radio
lunch
home
the car
a wath
a bus

8   Food

Match the words with the pictures.

olives	honey	chocolate
kebab	salad	potatoes
vegetables	rice	soup
eggs		

9 Write

Write these words in the sentences: **desert, beef, weather, menu, dinner, toy, lake, same, lamb, refinery, lesson**

a) The baby is playing with a new _____ .

b) Ahmed works in an oil _____ .

c) What time does the English _____ start?

d) _____ and _____ are both meat.

e) I'm having apple juice. Would you like the _____ ?

f) We always have picnics in the _____ in the winter.

g) I never swim in that _____ . The water is dirty.

h) Can I see the _____ please? We want something to eat.

i) The _____ is terrible today. Let's stay at home.

j) We usually have _____ at about seven o'clock in the evening.

10 Look and say

What's the time?   It's ... o'clock
It's half past ...
It's a quarter past/to ...
It's ... thirty/fifteen

a)   b)   c)   d)   e)   f)

g)   h)   i)   j)   k)   l)

PUNCTUATION

11 Write

Write the sentences with punctuation and capital letters.

a) i live in king faisal street _____

b) jawad goes to manama boys secondary school_____

c) theyre having lunch in the momtaz restaurant _____

d) adel and hamid arent going to doha today _____

e) its about seven oclock _____

f) tomorrow is national day in oman _____

g) were going to jebel akhdar for a picnic _____

h) samira doesnt study science she studies mathematics_____

i) mr and mrs brown dont speak arabic very well _____

J) we usually go to al hilal supermarket on thursdays _____

k) thats khalifas bag give it to him _____

l) it isnt raining now lets go out _____

SPELLING

12 Look

There are two spelling mistakes in every line.

a) A: Can I speek to Mr Parker, pleas?

b) B: I'm sarry. Mr Parker's busy. He's teeching.

c) A: At what time dose the leson finish?

d) B: It finishs at about twelve tharty.

e) A: I'll phone agin aftre the lesson.

f) C: What's the wether like todey, Fatima?

g) D: It's terible. It's cold and claudy.

h) C: It was beautifull yasterday.

i) D: Yes. It was suny and not too hat.

J) C: Let's stey at home and watsh a video.

k) D: Thet's a vary good idea!

PRONUNCIATION

13 Match

Match the words that have the same sounds.

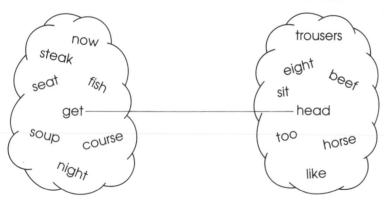

READ AND WRITE

14 Read

Read about Latifa's holiday.

a) Which city is Latifa in?
b) Where is Latifa going tomorrow?

Al Quds Hotel
King Hussein Street
Amman
Jordan

12.6.95

Dear Sarah,

Hello. How are you? I hope you are well.

I'm enjoying my holiday here in Jordan with my brother and my sister. We're staying in the Al Quds Hotel which is quite good and not very expensive. At the moment I am sitting in the hotel with my brother and writing this letter to you. The weather is very hot here in Amman and I am drinking a cold fruit juice! We were in the market this morning and it was very busy and very noisy.

We go to the market every morning. My sister loves shopping! She's got a lot of new dresses. In the evenings we usually visit my cousin, Muna. She's a student in the university here. She lives in a district of Amman called Shmeisani. It's quite a long way and so we take a taxi. This afternoon we're going to a museum not far from the hotel. Yesterday we went to a restaurant with my cousin. The food was terrible and so I don't feel very well this morning!

Tomorrow we are going to Damascus for a few days. I have another cousin in Damascus. His name's Ali and he works in the embassy. After that we will return to Amman and then fly back to Muscat

See you soon

Best wishes

Latifa

c) What is Latifa doing at the moment?
d) What is the weather like?
e) Where do they usually go in the evenings?
f) Where are they going this afternoon?
g) Where does Ali live?

15 Write

Join these sentences with **and then**. For example:

Tom has breakfast. He drives to work.
Tom has breakfast **and then** he drives to work.

a) Waleed has lunch at two o'clock. He goes to the club.
b) The English class finishes at four thirty. I drive home.
c) On Wednesday Fatima finishes work early. She visits her aunt in the hospital.
d) It usually rains in the morning. It is sunny in the afternoon.
e) We usually have a big lunch. We don't eat very much in the evening.
f) Rashid usually studies for two hours after dinner. He goes to bed.
g) You always look at my answers. You write them in your book!

16 Write

Write about the people in this picture. Use the verbs: **sit, have, look, drink, swim, walk, talk, listen, drive**

Begin: "Some people are having a picnic on the beach."

Khalid and his grandfather are at the end of their holiday in London. They are returning to Dubai tomorrow.

111

WORK BOOK

UNIT 1 At work

Lesson 1 A new job

1 Write

Have you _____ a driving _____?

No, I _____.

2 Numbers

Write the numbers.

13   _____

40   _____

68   _____

100   _____

530   _____

729   _____

1,000   _____

3 Match

Match the questions with the answers.

Is this car new?

Have you got a work permit?

Are you English?

Is Mary a teacher?

Has Omar got a passport?

Am I late?

No, I haven't.

Yes, I am.

Yes, you are.

No, it isn't.

Yes, she is.

Yes, he has.

4 Punctuation

Write these sentences with punctuation and capital letters.

a) have you got an egyptian visa

_____

b) doha isnt near muscat

_____

c) i havent got a syrian passport

_____

d) where is ahmed from

_____

e) i was born in salt in jordan

_____

f) were you born in saudi arabia

_____

g) is poona in pakistan

_____

h) no it isnt its in india

_____

5 Listen and write

| NAME: |
| NATIONALITY: |
| BORN: |
| JOB: |

6 Read

Use a dictionary.

Who am I?

a)

I am a woman. I am Lebanese and I was born in Beirut in Lebanon.
I am a famous singer.

b) A/W Silouhette of a man - head and shoulders.

I am a man. I was born in Brazil. I was a famous footballer, but now I am a business-man. I am quite rich.

c)

I am a man. I am Egyptian and I was born in Cairo. I was a student at Cairo University and now I am writer. I am an old man now.

d)

I am dead now. I was a famous actor and I was very funny. I was born in London, but my nationality was American.

Who are they: Charlie Chaplin, Fayrouz, Pele, Naguib Mahfouz.

7 Write

My name's Ahmed Hassan. I am twenty-seven years old. I am a driver. I was born in Aleppo in Syria.

Now write about you.

_____

_____

_____

Lesson 2 What's your address?

1 Write the address

Egypt

P.O.Box 73,

Cairo,

Mrs Salwa Jameel,

Heliopolis

_____

_____

_____

_____

_____

2 Months

a) J ___ n ___ ___ ry

b) ___ ___ br ___ ___ ry

c) M ___ rc ___

d) ___ pr ___ l

e) M ___ y

f) J ___ n ___

3 Write the year

1996   = nineteen _____

1997   = _____

1998   = _____

1999   = _____

2000   = two thousand

2001   = two thousand and one

2002   = _____

4 Days of the week

a) W ___ dn ___ sd ___ y

b) ___ r ___ ___ ay

c) S ___ t ___ rd ___ y

d) ___ h ___ rs ___ ___ ___

e) T ___ e ___ d ___ ___

f) S ___ n ___ ___ y

g) ___ o ___ d ___ y

Now write the days in order.

Saturday

_____

5 Listen

Listen and tick the numbers you hear.

a) 15 ☐   50 ☐   e) 417 ☐   470 ☐
b) 19 ☐   90 ☐   f) 814 ☐   840 ☐
c) 113 ☐   130 ☐   g) 1,916 ☐   1,960 ☐
d) 218 ☐   280 ☐

6 Read

Look at these two addresses.

Name/Company:	Mr. J. Main,	ITC Ltd.,
P.O.Box/Street:	52, Old Street,	P.O.Box 435,
Suburb/District:	Chelsea,	First Circle,
City:	London,	Amman,
Country:	United Kingdom	Jordan

7 What's your address?

ADDRESS
NAME: _____
ADDRESS: _____
_____
_____
_____

Lesson 3   **This is our office**

1 Write

And_____this_____desk?

No, that's_____desk. Look out! He's here.

DIRECTOR   MR J. KHALILI

116

2 Months

Write the months.

a) RECTOOB   _____

b) CEDEMREB   _____

c) YULJ   _____

d) GUSTAU   _____

e) VEMREBNO   _____

f) TEMSEPBRE   _____

3 Dates

Match the dates.

11th, 12th, 13th, 14th, 15th, 16th, 17th, 18th, 19th, 20th

fifteenth eighteenth twentieth eleventh fourteenth nineteenth seventeenth thirteenth sixteenth twelfth

4 Spelling

Find the correct spellings.

computer   computor, cumputer, computr, computer, conputre
filing   filling, filing, fileing, fling, filign
cabinet   cebinet, cabnet, cabinat, cibinet, cabinet
typewriter   typwriter, tipewriter, tyepwriter, typewriter, typewritre
telephone   telephon, tellefon, telephone, teliphone, tiliphon
shelf   shilf, shefl, shelf, shalf, shelfe
uniform   unform, unifirm, oniform, unifrm, uniform

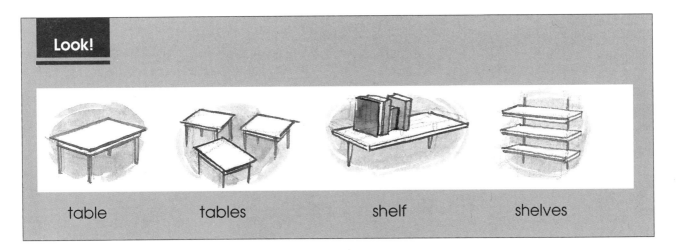

Look!

table   tables   shelf   shelves

5 Read

Our office is quite big. There's a desk on the left near the window and there's a desk on the right near the door. In the middle is a table. There's a computer on the table. On the wall near the door are some shelves. There are two filing cabinets below the shelves. There are two telephones in the office. One is on the table and the other is on the desk near the window.

a)   Where is the table?
b)   Where are the shelves?
c)   Where are the telephones?

Draw the **table, shelves** and **telephones** in the picture.

6 Write

There is	a ...	near
		next to
there are	two ...	on
	some ...	between ... and ...

a)
There is a telephone on the desk.

b)

c)

d)

e)

1 Write

Can I _____ your _____ please?

I'm very_____. I _____ got a pass.

2 Find

Find the word that is different.

a)   certificate, pass, job, diploma, permit, licence
b)   stop, come, wait, go, here
c)   day, week, February, month, year
d)   town, city, park, suburb, village, country
e)   desk, office, computer, table, chair, filing cabinet
f)   cap, uniform, overalls, jacket, hat, guard
g)   write, stamp, letter, envelope, address

3 Punctuation

Write these sentences with punctuation and capital letters.

a)   whats your address

_____

b)   its near the door

_____

c)   thats ahmeds locker

_____

d)   can i see your permit please

_____

e)   i was born on the third of january

_____

f)   is today tuesday or wednesday

_____

g)   ive got a yemeni passport

_____

4 Write

Write the dates in full.

12/10/68   12th October 1968

a) 21/5/89   _____

b) 3/9/95   _____

c) 17/11/75   _____

d) 2/4/68   _____

e) 30/8/93   _____

5 Write

Write the words in the correct order.

a) passport / me / please / your / show

_____

b) here / minute / please / wait / a

_____

c) not / I / a / permit / have / work / got

_____

d) see / licence / your / I / please / can / driving / ?

_____

e) desk / your / there / that's / over

_____

f) cabinet / this / my / is / filing / ?

_____

g) computer / is / that / Salwa's

_____

6 Dictation

_____

_____

_____

_____

7 Write

What are these signs?

a) _ _   _ _ _ _ _ _ _
b) _ _   _ _ _ _ _ _ _
c) _ _ _ _
d) _ _ _ _
e) _ _ _ _
f) _ _ _ _ _ _ _

8 Crossword

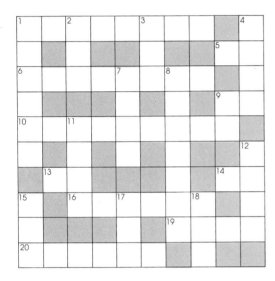

Across

1   The last month (8 letters).
5   Show_____your driving licence please. (2)
6   1995 =_____ninety-five. (8)
9   "Where's my filing cabinet?" " _____ s over there." (2)
10

(9)
13   There_____an old cupboard near the door. (2)
14   Mr Patel was born in India._____ is Indian. (2)
16   June, July, _____, September (6)

19

(4)

20   8th (6)

Down

1   Eat your_____, please (6)
2   _____I see your visitor's pass, please? (3)
3
"I'm tired!" "Have a _____." (4)
4   "I'm tired!" "Have a _____." (4)
7   Not short (4)
8   This bus is fast. It is an_____bus. (7)
9   _____this my desk? (2)
11   Have you got an Egyptian_____in your passport? (4)
12   _____you born in Lebanon? (4)
15   "Show me your indentity card, please." "Yes. Here you_____." (3)
17   Mary hasn't_____a Jordanian driving licence. (3)
18   Mary's desk is near_____window. (3)

UNIT 2 At home

1 Match

Match the verbs with the pictures.

Stand up. Sit down. Come in. Go out.

2 Spelling

Find the two correct spellings.

biscuit   bascuit, bisciut, biscuit, bscuit, biscut, biscuit.
cake   caek, cake, caik, cak, cayk, caek, cake, kace
coffee   cofee, caffee, caffe, coffe, coffee, cffee, coffee, coofee
milk   milik, milk, malik, malk, milk, mikl, mailk, mlik
sugar   sagar, suger, sugar, sugra, suger, sagra, sagur, sugar
would   wuld, woudl, would, woud, wood, wuld, would, woold
like   laik, lake, lyke, like, liek, liyek, leke, like
delicious   delicous, delisious, delicious, delicius, dellicous, delicious, dilicious

Look!

some / a

some coffee   **a** cup of coffee

3 Write

Write **some**, **a** or **an**.

a) I've got _____ sweet oranges.

b) Have _____ apple.

c) Mary's got _____ new job.

d) There are _____ shelves near the window.

e) Would you like _____ cup of coffee?

f) Saleem's got _____ good friends.

g) Have _____ seat.

h) There's _____ old filing cabinet next to the door.

i) Would you like _____ milk?

4 Write

Write the words in the correct lists.

water, apple, petrol, countries, chair, cup, people, juice, children, taxi, tea, cars

a / an	some	some
table	books	coffee
_____	_____	_____
_____	_____	_____
_____	_____	_____
_____	_____	_____

5 Read

a) Where are Latifa and her visitor? Put an X on the picture.

Latifa's House

Latifa's house is quite new. It is in a suburb of Kuwait called Salmiya. There are four rooms on the ground floor, a sitting room, a kitchen, a small dining room and a bathroom. Upstairs there are two bedrooms, one is large and the other is small. There is also another bathroom. Latifa has a visitor at the moment, her friend Sarah. They are having coffee in the sitting room.

Put a tick (✓) or a cross (✗)

b) Latifa's house is old.   ( )
c) It has two bedrooms.   ( )
d) There are two bathrooms.   ( )
e) The dining room is large.   ( )

6 Dictation

Listen and write.

_____

_____

_____

_____

7 Write

Number these sentences in the right order.

a) Would you like some tea? ☐   d) Sugar? ☐
b) No, thank you. ☐   e) Thanks. ☐
c) Come in Salwa. Have a seat. ☐   f) Yes, please. ☐

Lesson 2   Some more coffee?

1 Write

"I'd _____ another _____ of Cola please.

'Thanks.'

Goodbye.

That man is very quiet.

2 Write

Write: **am, is** or **are. ('m, 's, 're)**

a) They _____ delicious.
b) "Where _____ Taif?"
c) "It _____ near Jeddah."
d) " _____ you hungry?"
e) "No, thanks. I _____ full."
f) "That _____ enough, thank you."
g) There _____ two telephones in the office.

h) "An apple? Here you _____ ."
i) Nura _____ from Syria.
j) " _____ we late?"
k) "Yes, you _____ ."
l) Khalid and Abdullah _____ Egyptian.
m) I _____ very sorry.
n) This _____ our office.

3 Write

Put some more or another in these sentences.

a) Have _____ rice.
b) Would you like _____ cup of tea?
c) I think I'll have _____ apricot.
d) Can I have _____ salad, please?

e) I'd like _____ glass of milk please.
f) There are _____ biscuits in the kitchen.

4 Food and drink

Find these words.

a) MLKI   _____
c) REDAB   _____
e) LADAS   _____
g) ENCKICH   _____
i) TERWA   _____

b) EEFCOF   _____
d) AETM   _____
f) CEJIU   _____
h) CEIR   _____
j) EAT   _____

Now write them in the lists.

FOOD

_____

_____

_____

_____

_____

DRINK

_____

_____

_____

_____

_____

5 Write

Write in the pronouns: **I, you, he, she, it, we, they**

a) This is my sister, Miriam. _____ is a teacher in a primary school.

b) Hassan has got two children. _____ are called Jameela and Mohsin.

c) I was born in Broumana. _____ is a small town not far from Beirut.

d) "Would _____ like some more rice, Mohsin?"

    "No, thanks. That's enough. _____ am full."

e) Mohammad is Omani. _____ is an engineer in the oil company.

f) We are late. _____ 's six o'clock.

g) These typewriters are old. _____ are broken.

h) My husband and I are from Damascus. _____ are Syrian.

6 Read

a) What is the name of Hassan's wife?

This is Hassan's hotel. It's called the Good Luck Hotel. It's quite old but it is cheap and clean. There are three floors and fifteen bedrooms. There are two bathrooms on each floor and there's a small restaurant on the ground floor. There is also a lift, but it's not working at the moment. Hassan is the manager and he lives in the hotel with his wife, Aida, and their two children. They have just two rooms on the ground floor. It's not a very big place, but Hassan says: "It's our home."

Put a tick (✓) or a cross (X).

b) The hotel has fifteen bedrooms.
c) There are six bathrooms in the hotel.
d) Hassan's family live on the ground floor.

Look!

The cakes are **delicious**.   They are **delicious** cakes.
The hotel is **cheap**.   It's a **cheap** hotel.

Lesson 3   I like hot weather

1

"I _____ Mars very _____."   "Me _____ ! Let's go home."

2 Spelling

Find the two correct spellings.

summer   sumer, summar, summer, summre, sommer, sumre, summer, smmer.

winter   winter, wintre, winiter, winter, wanter, wantre, winater

cold   cald, colde, cold, culd, coled, code, cole, cold

weather   wether, weather, weathre, weathr, weather, weahter, waither

another   anather, an other, anothre, anether, another, another annother

some   soem, some, sume, soom, some, seem, som

enough   enough, enouhg, enuogh, enouf, anough, enough, ennugh

126

3 Write

Put the words in the right order.

a) like / summer / much / very / the / I

_____

b) cold / I / don't / weather / like

_____

c) winter / is / very / in / London / cold / the

_____

d) English / speak / do / very well / you / ?

_____

e) glass / would /a / milk / you / of / like / ?

_____

Look!

| the winter | the summer |
| in the winter, | in the summer. |

4 Write

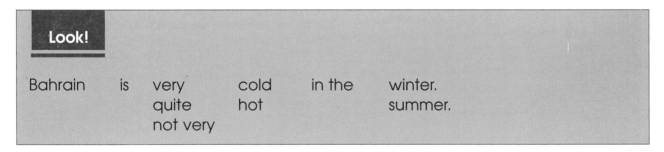

Look!

Bahrain	is	very	cold	in the	winter.
		quite	hot		summer.
		not very			

Write sentences like this:

Bahrain is quite cold in the winter

Write about:

a) Cairo   b) Riyadh   c) Muscat   d) Beirut   e) Your city/village

_____

_____

_____

_____

_____

5 Listen

Listen and circle the dates you hear.

	JUNE				JULY				AUGUST				
Saturday		6	13	20	27	4	11	18	25	1	8	15	22	29
Sunday			7	14	21	28	5	12	19	26	2	9	16	23	30
Monday	1	8	15	22	29	6	13	20	27	3	10	17	24	31
Tuesday	2	9	16	23	30	7	14	21	28	4	11	18	25
Wednesday	3	10	17	24	1	8	15	22	29	5	12	19	26
Thursday	4	11	18	25	2	9	16	23	30	6	13	20	27
Friday	5	12	19	26	3	10	17	24	31	7	14	21	28

6 Write

Write **in, on** or **at** in the sentences.

a)   He's from Sfax _____ Tunisia.

b)   The computer is over there, _____ the table.

c)   I'm afraid he's busy _____ the moment.

d)   I don't like Cairo _____ the summer. It's too hot for me.

e)   There are two shops _____ the right.

f)   Latifa is _____ home. She is _____ the kitchen.

g)   There's a desk _____ the middle of the room.

7 Write

Write some or any in these sentences.

a)   Have you got _____ biscuits?

b)   I'd like _____ rice.

c)   Peter hasn't got _____ pictures in his classroom.

d)   There are _____ books on the shelves.

e)   I'm sorry. There isn't _____ orange juice. But I've got _____ lemonade.

f)   We haven't got _____ petrol!

8 Read

a)   Which floor is Salwa's apartment on?

My family and I have an apartment in a building called the
Kuwaiti Building. It is in the centre of Manama in a district
called Gudabiya. I like this area because it is near to the
shops and its also near my work. I am a secretary in an
airline company. The apartment is quite big. It has three
bedrooms and two bathrooms. It is a nice apartment, but
I don't like it very much. It is on the twelfth floor
and I am afraid of heights!

b)   Where is Salwa's apartment?
c)   Is it small?
d)   What is Salwa's job?

Lesson 4   **I like cooking**

1 Listen and tick (✓)

a)	thin ☐	thing ☐	e)	ban ☐	bang ☐
b)	thin ☐	thing ☐	f)	ban ☐	bang ☐
c)	thin ☐	thing ☐	g)	ban ☐	bang ☐
d)	thin ☐	thing ☐	h)	ban ☐	bang ☐

Question:	What's this game?
Answer:	ping-pong (or, table-tennis)

2 Listen and say

A: What's that thing?
B: What thing?
A: There. On the floor.
B: Hmm. It's interesting.
A: I think it's a ring.
B: A ring?
A: Yes. A wedding ring.
B: You're right. It is a ring.
   It's my wedding ring!

3 Punctuation

Write these sentences with punctuation and capital letters.

a) id like some milk please

b) i dont like swimming very much

c) do you like muscat

d) we havent got any pepsi

e) i think ill have some dates

f) can i have some bread please

g) thats enough milk

4 Find

Find the word that is different.

a) meat, chicken, rice, salad, food, bread
b) drink, water, milk, juice, lemonade, tea
c) January, September, May, Friday, April, October
d) why, who, how, what, this, where, whose
e) twelfth, eighteenth, second, thirty-first, twenty-third, seven
f) seat, stand up, come in, go out, wait, stop, sit down
g) walking, reading, swimming, cooking, interesting, driving

5 Match

Match the questions with the answers.

a) Where is the glass?
b) How old is Miriam?
c) What time is it?
d) How much is that radio?
e) Why are you late?
f) Who is that?
g) How is the coffee?
h) Whose is that?

1) Fine.
2) Because my wife is in the hospital.
3) It's on the table.
4) That's my cousin, Abdullah.
5) I think it's mine.
6) She's eleven.
7) It's nine o'clock.
8) Sixty-two dinars.

6 Hobbies

Ask six students about their hobbies. Ask:

Do you like ... ?

NAME	cooking	reading	playing sports	visiting relatives	watching TV	learning English	other
Latifa	✓	✓	✗	✓	✗	✓	learning French

7 Write

Write a, an, the, or (-) .

a) Can I have _____ glass of water, please?

b) I like London in _____ summer.

c) Have _____ seat.

d) That building is _____ National Commercial Bank.

e) Latifa is in _____ kitchen.

f) I think I'll have _____ orange.

g) They're _____ delicious cakes.

h) Your desk is on _____ left.

i) Do you like _____ swimming?

j) Can I speak to _____ manager, please?

k) There's _____ shop next to our building.

l) That's _____ old car.

8 Crossword

Across

1 The_____in Bahrain is quite nice in February. (7 letters)

5 My wife and I are from Bombay._____ are Indian. (2)

6 Come in, Zainab. Please_____ down. (3)

7 The_____in Riyadh is very hot. (6)

9 I do not = I don't; I would =_____ (2)

10 Not easy. (9)

12 Have some chicken_____ 's delicious! (2)

13 I like_____football on the television. (8)

16 What would you like, tea_____ coffee? (2)

17

STOP   WAIT   _____ (2)

19 No more bread, thanks. I've got_____ (6)

22 "Do you like reading?" No_____much. (3)

Down

1 _____you like another cup of coffee? (5)

2 12th (7)

3 That's my daughter. She's two years old and _____ name's Jawaher (3)

4 I like_____relatives on Saturday mornings. (8)

8 He's_____(6)

11 Sugar is_____(5)

14 "I like Cairo in winter." "Me_____." (3)

15 Yes and_____(2)

18

Go — (3)

20

(2)

21 This is Joe._____is from Toronto in Canada. (2)

UNIT 3 My life

I live in Doha

1 Write

2 Spelling

Find the Two correct spellings.

have	heve, haiv, have, hav, haev, hiav, have, hev
work	worek, werk, wark, work, wirik, work, worke, wurik
live	laiv, live, leiv, leav, laiv, liev, live, liv
study	stady, study, istudy, stedy, studie, stoudi, stdy, study
like	like, laik, leik, lick, lake, like, leik, layk
play	pelay, blay, pley, play, blae, plai, play, playe
learn	leren, learn, laern, learen, lairn, learn, learne, lairn

3 Write

Put the words in the right order.

a) flat / large / a / live / we / in

_____

b) company / work / a / for / big / I

_____

c) new / we / car / a / have

_____

d) live / school / you / the / do / near / ?

_____

e) don't / in / we / ministry / work / the

_____

133

f)   playing / you / basketball / do / like / ?

_____

g)   lot / have / a / free / I / of / don't / time

_____

> ### Look!
>
> **a / the**
>
> I work for **a** small company in Doha.
> The name of **the** company is
> ARK Limited.
>
> in **the** morning
> in **the** afternoon
> in **the** evening

4   Write

Write a, an or the.

I live in (a) _____ old house. (b) _____ house is quite near (c) _____ centre of
Aleppo. I am (d) _____ secretary and my husband is (e) _____ accountant. I work
in (f) _____ bank. (g) _____ name of (h) _____ bank is (i) _____ National
Commercial Bank. In (j) _____ afternoons I study English at (k) _____ British Council.

5   Punctuation

Write the sentences with punctuation and capital letters.

a)   i havent got much time

_____

b)   do you like playing tennis

_____

c)   we dont live in heliopolis we live in zemalik

_____

d)   i am a teacher and i live in beirut

_____

e)   do you work in the hilton hotel

_____

f)   nadia and latifa work in a hospital

_____

6   What am I?

Read about these animals. Use your dictionary, Then match the pictures with the paragraphs.

a)   I am very big. I live in Africa. I like eating leaves. I am grey and I have a thick coat and a long "nose" called a trunk. I also have big ears.

b)   I live in trees. I like eating bananas and other fruit. I have a long tail.

c)   I don't have any legs or arms. I am long and thin. I live in long grass or in the desert. I am dangerous!

d)   I live in the sea. I haven't got any arms or legs, but I've got a tail. I like swimming!

e)   I live in India. I am quite big and I am very fast. I have a beautiful coat. I don't eat grass. I eat small animals. I am dangerous too!

f)   I am a good worker. I work a lot. I live in the desert and I carry things for people. Sometimes people sit on my back. I am strong.

7 Write

You are Yasser or Habiba. Write a paragraph. Begin: My name's ...

Name:	Yasser Abdul Qader
Born:	Beirut Year: 1973
Live:	Amman – Jordan
Job:	businessman
Company:	father's company
Free time:	swimming, playing table-tennis

Name:	Habiba Al-Husseini
Born:	Hofuf – Year: 1968 Saudi Arabia
Live:	Riyadh
Job:	teacher – primary school
Free time:	reading, cooking

_____

_____

_____

_____

_____

_____

Lesson 2   Where do you work?

1 Listen and tick

a) sit ☐   seat ☐
b) sit ☐   seat ☐
c) sit ☐   seat ☐
d) sit ☐   seat ☐
e) sit ☐   seat ☐
f) sit ☐   seat ☐
g) sit ☐   seat ☐
h) sit ☐   seat ☐

2 Write

Put the words in the right order to make questions.

a) company / do / for / you / which / work / ?

_____

b) you / do / live / where / ?

_____

c) do / what / do / you / ?

_____

d) the centre / you / near / do / live / ?

_____

e) you / Yemen / are / from / ?

_____

f) like / you / languages / do / learning / ?

_____

g) country / from / you / which / are / ?

_____

h) a flat / live / you / do / in / ?

_____

3 Match

Match the questions above with the answers.

1) (India.)

2) (No. I'm from Saudi Arabia.)

3) (In Amman.)

4) (No. We have a small house.)

5) (I'm a businessman)

6) (No. In a suburb.)

7) (BAPCO.)

8) (No. Not much.)

4 Jobs

Find the jobs. Match them to the pictures.

a) p __ l __ t

b) c __ sh __ __ r

c) st __ w __ __ d

d) ac __ __ __ nt __ __ __

e) n __ r __ __

f) m __ ch __ n __ __

g) b __ s __ n __ __ __ m __ n

h) d __ __ t __ __

i) __ __ x __ dr __ __ __ __

j) g __ __ rd

5 Write

Write **in, at, for** or **from** in these sentences.

a) I work ____ my brother.

b) He's got a restaurant ____ Amman.

c) Sam's American. He's ____ Dallas ____ Texas.

d) We work ____ an office. We're secretaries.

e) I study English ____ the afternoons.

f) Do you work ____ the airport?

g) I was born ____ 1995.

h) Latifa and her family are ____ home.

6 Read

Read about Aziza and Simon.

My name's Aziza. I live in Amman in a suburb. I am twenty years old and I am single. I live with my parents and my brothers and sisters. I was born in Saudi Arabia, but I am Jordanian. I work for the Ministry of Foreign Affair in Amman. I'm a secretary. I like my job because it's quite interesting. In my free time I like reading and visiting friends and relatives. I also like shopping.

My name's Simon Star. I am American. I was born in New York in 1967 but I live in Los Angeles now. I don't work - I play basketball! I play for the Los Angeles Jets and I am a famous player. I have a wife and two small children. We have a house by the sea not far from Los Angeles. I travel a lot. I visit many different countries. I don't have time for a lot of hobbies, but I like swimming and sitting in the sun.

Now fill in their identification cards.

```
Name: _____          Name: _____
Born: _____ Year: _____  Born: _____ Year: _____
Live: _____          Live: _____
Job: _____           Job: _____
Hobbies/                        Hobbies/
Free time: _____      Free time: _____
       _____                 _____
```

7 Write

Now write about your life! First write in the information. Then write a paragraph.

```
Name: _____
Born: _____ Year: _____
Live: _____
Job: _____
Hobbies/Free time: _____
_____
```

Lesson 3 My children go to school

1 Spelling

Find the subjects.

Subjects	
a) ABICAR	a) _____
b) GLIHSEN	b) _____
c) CESCINE	c) _____
d) TORHISY	d) _____
e) CHFERN	e) _____
f) TICSMAMETHA	f) _____

2 Spelling

Find the *two* correct spellings.

whicf	witch, whish, which, hwich, whech, which, wiche, watch
what	whet, what, hwat, whot, wath, what, wate, wat
where	weyre, whayr, wheer, whear, where, were, where, wheir
why	hwy, whi, why, wye, way, why, wey, whi
who	woh, how, who, whu, huw, hwo, who, how
whose	whoos, whoze, whose, whoes, hwose, whuse, house, whose
how	hwo, haw, who, huw, how, howe, tow, how

3 Punctuation

Write out these sentences with punctuation and capital letters.

a)   do your children go to al awal secondary school

_____

b)   fawzia and omar study at cairo university

_____

c)   we dont go to school on fridays

_____

d)   i like studying french and arabic

_____

Look!

Yes / no questions		Do you	live ... ?	**Yes**, I do.
			like	**No**, I don't.
Are you ... ?	**Yes**, I am.		work	
	No, I'm not.		study	
			go	

---

4 Questions

This is Wendy. She is Sam's sister and she is in Cairo at the moment. Ask her questions. Use:

Are you ... ?
or:
Do you + verb ... ?

a)   from / Dallas ?

_____

b)   British or American ?

_____

c)   like / Cairo ?

_____

d) live / Egypt ?

_____

e) a teacher ?

_____

f) speak / Arabic ?

_____

g) work / Dallas ?

_____

5 Listen

Listen and circle the numbers you hear.

a)	116	160	260	616	106	16
b)	953	539	583	533	935	593
c)	742	472	724	427	704	720
d)	417	470	47	407	704	447
e)	903	913	530	390	930	130
f)	650	695	659	609	965	615
g)	200	1,000	1,002	2,000,000	200,000	2,000

6 Listen and write

_____

_____

_____

_____

_____

_____

7 Write

Join the sentences with **and** or **but**.

For example:

I am a doctor. I work in the International Hospital.
I am a doctor **and** I work in the International Hospital.

Nadia and Samira like school. They don't like their teacher.
Nadia and Samira like school **but** they don't like their teacher.

a)   I was born in Oman. I live in Abu Dhabi now.

   _____

b)   I am a bus driver. I work for Express Transport Company.

   _____

c)   My brothers live in Sharjah. They work in Dubai.

   _____

d)   My sister and I study English. We speak it quite well.

   _____

e)   Mr Barry is from Oxford. His wife is from Leeds.

   _____

f)   Tom and Mary like listening to the radio. They don't like watching television.

   _____

g)   I am a basketball player. I play for Cairo All Stars.

   _____

Lesson 4   **Peter's school**

1 Write

_____ the window, please, Khalid.
It's very _____ in here.

142

2 Spelling

a) Have you got a w ___ tc ___ ?

b) This lesson is b ___ r ___ ng!

c) How much m ___ n ___ y do you have in your pocket?

d) Are those your car k ___ ___ s or mine?

e) It's very q ___ ___ ___ t in the room. Where is everyone?

f) The engine is very n ___ ___ sy.

g) Can I see your h ___ m ___ w ___ ___ ___ , please?

3 Write

Put the words in the correct order.

a) me / your / pen / please / give

_____

b) Latifa / that / show / letter

_____

c) your / him / give / address

_____

d) guard / your / show /visitor's / the / pass

_____

e) money / cashier / the / the / give

_____

f) new / her / your / flat / show

_____

4 Punctuation

Write the paragraph with punctuation and capital letters.

my names nora im from iraq and im a student at baghdad university i study medicine i live in a suburb of baghdad with my family i have three brothers and one sister i speak arabic english and some french my brothers are quite young and they go to school my sister is a teacher.

_____

_____

_____

_____

_____

5 Match the words

Verbs

come   close
open   (stop)   (go)   love
sit   stand
    hate
push   pull
    go

Adjectives

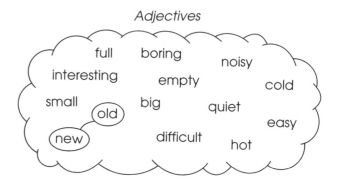

        full   boring   noisy
interesting   empty   cold
small   big   quiet
    (old)   easy
(new)   difficult   hot

6 Read

What are they?

These animals aren't very big, but they aren't very small. They have four legs and two horns. They have long hair which is brown, black or grey. They also have beards. They live in many different countries. They eat grass and leaves from trees, but they don't eat other animals. They don't work for man, but they give us milk and meat.

They are _____.

What're their jobs?

These people give us food and drink, but they don't work in hotels or in restaurants. They work in different countries. Sometimes they work between countries! They have a busy life. Their job is tiring and sometimes dangerous, but they are always happy and smiling!

They are _____ and _____.

144

7 Write

Read about Tariq and Hamid. Put these verbs in the paragraph: **hate, go, have, play, study, like, like, are, live**

Tariq and Hamid (a) _____ my friends. They (b) _____ a sister called Layla, and they all (c) _____ with their parents in a suburb of Kuwait called Safat. Tariq and Hamid (d) _____ to Kuwait University. They both (e) _____ engineering and mathematics. They (f) _____ engineering very much, but they (g) _____ mathematics. They think it's very difficult. In their free time Tariq and Hamid (h) _____ many different sports - basketball, football and table-tennis. They also (i) _____ driving to the sea and visiting friends and relatives.

8 Crossword

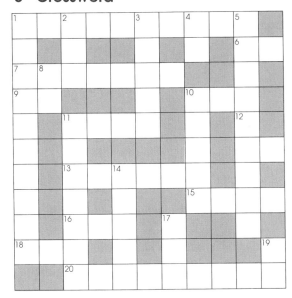

Across

1 Flats. (10 letters)
6 A famous film about a visitor from space! (1,1)
7 ARAMCO is a large oil_____. (7)
9 Heliopolis is a suburb_____Cairo. (2)
10 _____are you? (3) "I'm khalifa."
11 Latifa and Habiba are from Sur, but —- live in Kuwait. (4)
12 "What do you_____ ?" "I'm a nurse." (2)
13 From Morocco to Oman people speak this language. (6)

15 and 16. "Is this Nadia's handbag?" "Yes, it's _____." (4) "Give it to_____, please." (3)
18 They study English in_____evening. (3)
20 Cousins, aunts, uncles, brothers and sisters are all_____. (9)

Down

1 "What's your job?" "I'm an_____." (10)
2  (3)
3   (5)
4 "Do you live in Riyadh?" "_____, we don't. We live in Jeddah." (2)
5 Awad and Tariq are sixteen. They go to_____school. (9)
8 The name_____the bank is the Commercial Bank. (2)
10 " _____car would you like - this one or that one?" (5)
11 Peter Parker is a _____in Capital English School. (7)
14 The month after March. (5)
17 Simon Star is rich. He has a_____of money. (3)
19 "Is that your book?" "Yes, it_____. (2)

UNIT 4 Family and Friends

Lesson 1   My brother lives in Beirut

1 Write

Write likes or like.

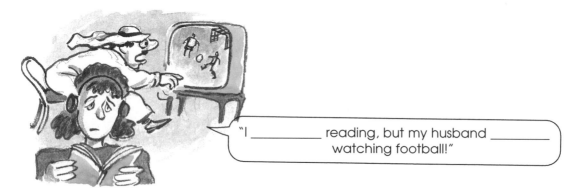

"I _____ reading, but my husband _____ watching football!"

2 Spelling

Find the two correct spellings.

goes   geos, goes, gose, goze, geos, goes, goos, goss

studies   stadies, studys, studes, studies, stodies, studyes, studies stidies

teaches   teechs, teachs, teache, teaches, teeches, teachs, teaches teashes

plays   pleys, blays, playes, pleyes, pelays, plays, plaes, plays

watches   watchs, watchis, watches, waches, watshes, wetches,

works   werks, workes, woreks, works, wirks, works, workis warks

catches   catchs, caches, catches, cetches, catche, catshes, catches, cashes

3 Write

Write sentences with **but**.

Example: I work in an office, but my wife works in a hospital.

a)   I / work / Sharjah / my brother / Al Ain

_____

b)   We / study / English / our sister / German

_____

c)   Tom and Mary / like / the market / their son / the park

_____

d)   I / teach / French / my wife / Arabic

_____

e) My husband and I / live / Aqaba / my father / Amman

_____

f) Waleed and Mustafa / play / table-tennis / Jameel / basketball

_____

g) My sisters / go / primary school / brother / intermediate school

_____

4 Listen

Listen and write about Abdullah.

Name: _____
Born: _____ Date: _____
Live: _____
Job: _____
Company: _____
Hobbies / Free time: _____
_____

5 Write

Write was or were in the dialogue.

A: Are you Emirati?
B: Yes, I am.
A: (a) _____ you born in the Emirates?
B: Yes. I (b) _____ born in Dubai.
A: And your wife too?
B: No. She (c) _____ born in Al-Ain.
A: So you (d) _____ born in Dubai but your wife (e) _____ born in Al-Ain.
B: That's right.
A: And where (f) _____ your father born?
B: In Dubai.

6 Read and write

Write in the verbs.

My friend, Ahmed, (a) _____ born in Homs in Syria, but he (b) _____ in Damascus

now. He (c) _____ in a small company called Al-Sham Trading. In his free time he

(d) _____ visiting friends and relatives. On Tuesday evenings he (e) _____ English.

Sometimes he (f) _____ volleyball with his friends. He is married and he (g)

_____ one child.

7 Write

Write about a friend. Use these verbs: **was born, lives, works, likes, studies, has (has got), goes**

_____

_____

_____

_____

_____

_____

Lesson 2   A wedding party

1 Write

Who's that funny man?

_____ one?

The _____ in the black cap.

2 Questions

Put the words in the correct order.

a)   she / live / in / Jordan / does / ?

_____

b)   Tawfiq / where / does / work / ?

_____

c)   they / studying / like / English / do / ?

_____

d)   does / Gary / what / do / ?

_____

e)   languages / speak / do / many / you / ?

_____

f) your / play / brother / basketball / does / ?

_____

g) hate / you / do / why / driving / ?

_____

3   Spelling

What are these clothes?

a) tr __ __ s __ rs   b) sk __ __ __
c) d __ __ ss   d) __ h __ __ t
e) s __ __ es   f) __ __ ck __ t
g) c __ __   h) s __ __ t

> **Look!**
>
> **Let's** ...   **Let's** ask Kamila.
>   **Let's** have a cup of coffee.
> **Let's** = let us   **Let's** go!

4   Punctuation

Write the sentences with punctuation and capital letters.

a) whos that man

_____

b) miriam doesnt live in baghdad

_____

c) does ahmed work for pdo

_____

d) toms very clever

_____

e) is kamila a lecturer

_____

f) they dont like visiting relatives

_____

g) lets ask mr brown

_____

5 Match

Match the questions with the answers.

a) Where does she work?
b) Do you like swimming
c) Is your car Japanese?
d) Why does he live in that district.
e) Does Fadhila live in an apartment?
f) Are you from Pakistan?
g) What does Peter do?
h) Which subject does she teach?

1) He's a teacher.
2) No, she doesn't.
3) No, I don't.
4) Yes, I am.
5) Because it's near his job.
6) In an office.
7) Science, I think.
8) Yes, it is.

Look!
also / too
Kamila speaks English.
She **also** speaks a little Turkish.
She speaks a little Turkish **too**.

Look!
both
Hassan and his brother **both** work in a restaurant.
They are **both** waiters.

6 Write

Put **also**, **too** or **both** in these sentences.

a) My friend is from Tokyo and I am from Osaka. We are Japanese. (both)

_____

b) I live in a suburb of Cairo. My sister lives in Cairo. (also)

_____

c) Tom likes reading in the evenings. He likes cooking. (too)

_____

d) My husband and I study at Qatar University. (both)

_____

e) Mike teaches English at the university. He teaches at the British Council in the evening. (also)

_____

f) My daughter goes to Karana Girls Primary School. My friend's daughter goes there. (too)

_____

7 Read

What are their jobs? Use a dictionary.

a) Tariq doesn't walk very much. He sits a lot and waits. He waits outside hotels, at the airport or at the bus station. Then he drives people from one place to another. They give him money. He's a _____.

b) Aziza works in an office with many people. Her job is quite interesting. She does many different things. She speaks to people on the telephone. She also writes letters for her boss. She uses a typewriter or a computer. She's a _____.

c) Mustapha works in a hotel. But he doesn't work in reception and he doesn't work in the kitchen. He meets many people during the day. They are usually hungry or thirsty! He brings them food and drink. He's a _____.

d) Samia speaks to thousands of people every day and thousands of people see her. They like listening to her because she tells them about important things. She also tells them about the weather. She is on television for twenty minutes every evening. She's a _____.

Lesson 3   Shopping

1 Write

2 Find the colours

a) LUBE _____

b) WELLYO _____

c) SLIVRE _____

d) NERGE _____

e) CKABL _____

f) ETIWH _____

g) YERG _____

h) DRE _____

i) NROWB _____

j) NKIP _____

k) GENORA _____

l) LODG _____

3 Write

Write **do** or **does** in these questions.

a) _____ you speak Arabic?

b) _____ Miriam work in Cairo?

c) Where _____ Bob and Ann live?

d) How much _____ those trousers cost?

e) Which school _____ Khalid go to?

f) What _____ you do?

g) _____ I speak Urdu? No, just a few words.

h) How much _____ that video recorder cost?

4 Write

Write **don't** or **doesn't** in these sentences.

a) What do you mean? We _____ understand.

b) Salwa _____ teach in a primary school.

c) Mr and Mrs Brown _____ live in England now.

d) I _____ like that dress very much. It's awful!

e) Hassan _____ live in Syria. He lives in Egypt.

f) This car _____ cost very much. It's a bargain!

g) You _____ like geography or history and you _____ like science or mathematics. What do you like?

5 Read

Find the animal: **horse, dog, cat**. Use a dictionary.

a) In Britain this animal is a very popular. Many families have one. It lives with the family and guards the house. It eats meat. There are many different kinds. Some are very small, but some are quite big. They can be dangerous, but usually they are friendly.
It's a _____

b) This animal is also popular in Britain. It lives with families. It eats meat or fish and drinks milk. It looks like a tiger or a lion, but it is much smaller. it has a soft coat. It is a very clean animal. It loves washing itself!
It's a _____

c) This animal is quite large, so it doesn't live in the house. Its colour is brown, black or grey. It carries people on its back or sometimes it pulls a small cart. It runs very fast. It doesn't eat meat. It usually eats grass.
It's a _____

6 Listen

Tick (✓) the number you hear.

a)	1,840 ☐	1,480 ☐	1,804 ☐	1,814 ☐
b)	5,390 ☐	5,913 ☐	5,930 ☐	5,319 ☐
c)	807 ☐	8,700 ☐	8,070 ☐	870 ☐
d)	6,755 ☐	7,655 ☐	6,759 ☐	6,750 ☐
e)	616 ☐	6,060 ☐	6,016 ☐	660 ☐
f)	1,000 ☐	10 ☐	10,000 ☐	100 ☐
g)	4,238 ☐	2,438 ☐	238 ☐	4,038 ☐
h)	4,300 ☐	3,410 ☐	410 ☐	3,400 ☐

7 Write

Mary Brown is writing about two friends. Write in the missing verbs in the correct form,

My friends Zaheda and Amina (a) _____ (live) in the apartment next to ours. They (b) _____ (be) sisters. Zaheda (c) _____ (be) a student at the University of Jordan. She (d) _____ (study) French and Arabic. Amina (e) _____ (not study). She (f) _____ (be) a cashier and (g) _____ (work) in a bank near our building. Amina (h) _____ (like) her job, but Zaheda (i) _____ (not like) studying very much. I think her course (j) _____ (be) very difficult.

Zaheda and Amina (k) _____ (visit) me every evening and sometimes we (l) _____ (go) shopping in Amman. They (m) _____ (be) good friends I (n) _____ (like) them both very much.

Lesson 4   Congratulations

1 Dictation

Listen and write.

_____

_____

_____

_____

_____

_____

2 Find

a) dress, shirt, skirt, clothes, trousers, suit, jacket
b) pink, apple, red, green, orange, blue, brown
c) great, good, excellent, fantastic, big
d) pretty, clever, doctor, happy, nice, sweet
e) shopping, studying, walking, fishing, wedding, driving, playing
f) riyal, pound, price, dinar, dollar, dirham
g) horse, elephant, fish, dog, monkey, cat, camel, tiger, snake
h) Urdu, Farsi, Turkish, India, French, English, German, Arabic

3 Write

Write these sentences in their full form.

a) Waleed's got a new car.

_____

b) Sarah doesn't live in Bahrain.

_____

c) I'll phone again this afternoon.

_____

d) They don't speak Arabic.

_____

e) We've got a new English teacher.

_____

f) Fatima and Aziza aren't from Egypt.

_____

g) I'm from Jordan and my wife's from Iraq.

_____

h) I'd like a glass of water.

_____

4 Write

Write in the correct part of the verb **to be**: am **('m), are, is ('s)**

A: Excuse me. (a) _____ you Gary Jones?

B: Yes, I (b) _____ . Who (c) _____ you?

A: I (d) _____ Abdul Qader. Welcome to Abu Dhabi.

B: Thank you. But where (e) _____ Waleed and Khalid?

A: I'm sorry. They (f) _____ late.

B: That (g) _____ all right. Oh, this (h) _____ my wife, Susan.

C: How do you do?

A: Pleased to meet you. (i) _____ you from England too?

C: Yes. My husband and I (j) _____ both from London.

A: Look. I think that (k) _____ Waleed.

B: Yes, but where (l) _____ Khalid?

A: I don't know.

6 Dictionary
Put these verbs in alphabetical order (A, B, C, ...): **go, say, look, come, hate, have, ask, answer, write, read, visit, like, catch, teach**

answer

ask

_____   _____

_____   _____

_____   _____

_____   _____

_____   _____

7 Write

Find out about another student. Ask him / her:

Where do you live?
Do you live in a house or a flat?
Do you work? Where?
Where were you born?
What do you do in your free time?
Do you like learning English?

etc.

Now write a paragraph about your partner.

_____

_____

_____

_____

_____

8 Crossword

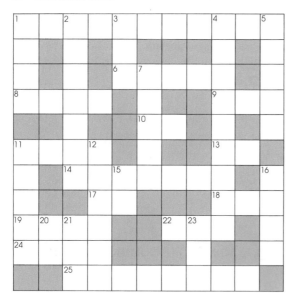

Across

1 He is married to my wife's mother. (6-2-3)

6

8 Those shirts cost two riyals —- . (4)

9 How many rooms has your house —- ? (3)

10 I'm tired. Let's —- home. (2)

11 —- your bother speak English? (4)

13 She studies —- the University of Khartoum. (2)

14 Simon Star is quite lazy. He likes —- in the sun. (7)

17 "Do you like fishing?" "—-,I don't." (2)

18 (3)

19 What a nice —- ! Sing it again! (4)

22 Gamel Abdul Nasser —- born in 1918. (3)

24 (4)

25  (8)

Down

1 Jameel has a busy life. He doesn't have much —- time. (4)

2 Peter is a good teacher. He —- very well. (7)

3 We are hungry and thirsty. Let's —- and drink. (3)

4 Arabic, Urdu, Turkish and German are all —- (9)

5 It's not black. (5)

7 Not left. (5)

11  (5)

12 Mohammad Abdu sings well. He's a good —- . (6)

15 She goes —- intermediate school. (2)

16 "I've got a new job." " —- done!" (4)

20  (2)

21 doesn't = does —- (3)

23 Where —- you from? (3)

UNIT 5 When?

Lesson 1   My day

1 Write

Write in the verbs: to finish, to catch.

_____ at four o'clock, but she _____ at three!

Look!

s / es
I start work at seven. I finish at six.
Ahmed start**s** work at seven. He
finishes at six.

watch**es**, catch**es**, teach**es**, finish**es**

My friend _____ large fish, but I only _____ small ones!

2 Write

Write five sentences from the table.

I	(usually)	start	work	early.
We	(sometimes)	finish	school	at ...
They			college	
Tariq		starts		
Noori		finishes		

_____

_____

_____

_____

_____

3 Spelling

Find the two correct spellings.

breakfast brakefast, breakfest, brakfast, breakfast, breekfst, preakfast, breakfast, breakfst

lunch lanch, lunsh, luntsh, lunch, lench, lunach, lunhc, lunch

dinner diner, drnner, dinner, dinnre, dinnar, dinar, dinner, denner

start staret, istart, start, stert, starat, start, estart, strat

finish finish, finnish, finsh, fanish, finich, finish

quarter quarter, quarter, quartre, quater, qwarter, qurter, quarter, qarter

4 Write

Write **in** or **at** in these sentences.

a) We live ____ a small house near the bus station.
b) Leyla starts work ___ half past seven.
c) My brother usually goes to his sports club ____ the evening.
d) Kamila and Jaber live ____ Jeddah.
e) Ahmed is ____ home at the moment.
f) I start work early ____ the morning.
g) Do you sometimes work ____ night?
h) My wife usually has breakfast ____ six o'clock.

5 Questions

Write in these question words: **why, whose, where, how much, who, what, when, which, how**

a) _____ do you usually have breakfast?
b) _____ does Ahmed work?
c) _____ is the woman in the red dress?
d) _____ country do you come from?
e) _____ is that bag over there?
f) _____ are you today, Hamid?
g) _____ is your address?
h) _____ do you hate playing table-tennis?

6 Match

Now match the question above with the answers.

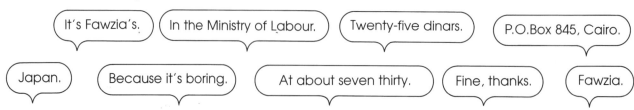

It's Fawzia's. In the Ministry of Labour. Twenty-five dinars. P.O.Box 845, Cairo.

Japan. Because it's boring. At about seven thirty. Fine, thanks. Fawzia.

<table>
<tr><td colspan="2">Look!</td></tr>
<tr><td colspan="2">work</td></tr>
<tr><td>Verb: to work</td><td>I work in an office.</td></tr>
<tr><td>Noun: work</td><td>I start work at eight o'clock.
The work is hard.
It is interesting work.</td></tr>
</table>

7 Listen and write

Nadia is talking about her day in the hospital. Write in the times.

	TIME
start work	_____
finish work	_____
breakfast	_____
lunch	_____
dinner	_____

Lesson 2   What do you have for breakfast?

1 Write

Write **usually, sometimes** or **never**.

I _____ walk under ladders, Ali. It's bad luck.

159

2 Spelling

```
┌─────────────────────────────────────────────┐
│            BREAKFAST                          │
│   a) c h _ _ s _                              │
│   b) t _ _ _                                  │
│   c) o _ _ v _ s                              │
│   d) b r _ _ _ _                              │
│   e) c _ f f _ _                              │
│   f) d _ t _ _                                │
│   g) y _ g h _ _ _ _                          │
│   h) j _ _ _                                  │
│    i) _ _ g s                                 │
│   j) o r _ _ g _   j _ _ c e _                │
└─────────────────────────────────────────────┘
```

3 Times

Write out the times.

a) *half past three*
or three thirty

b) _____

c) **8:45** _____

d) **11:15** _____

e) _____

f) _____

g) _____

h) MONDAY   **9 4 5**   **2 1** _____

i) **7:15** _____

4 Punctuation

Write out this paragraph in sentences (four) with punctuation and capital letters.

najwa gets up at six oclock she usually has milk bread and jam for breakfast and she sometimes has an egg najwa works for the commercial bank in muscat she starts work at eight oclock and she finishes at three

_____

_____

_____

_____

5 Write

Put the words in the correct order.

a) you / up / do / usually / when / get / ?

_____

b) khalifa / time / work / start / what / does / ?

_____

c) your children / for /have / what / breakfast / do / ?

_____

d) early / Latifa / have / does / breakfast / ?

_____

e) finish / when / Ahmed / work / does / ?

_____

f) usually / early /up / they / get / do / ?

_____

Now put these words in the correct order.

g) up / never / we / late / get

_____

h) chicken / I / sometimes / lunch / for / have

_____

i) evening / Bashir / the / never / in / studies

_____

j) doesn't /on Friday / brother / work / my / usually

_____

6 Read

Read about Hanan's morning. Use a dictionary. Answer the questions.

My morning

I always get up early. I pray and then I prepare breakfast for the family. We usually have eggs, tea, bread and cheese or honey. The children drink milk. My husband goes to work at seven thirty and then I take the children to school. School starts at eight o'clock. After that I return home, or sometimes I go shopping with my friend, Miriam. She lives next door.

a) What do the family have for breakfast?
b) Do the children have tea?
c) When does Hanan's husband go to work?
d) What time does school start?
e) Who is Miriam?

7 Write

Write about your day. When do you get up? What do you have for breakfast? When do you start work / school? When do you finish?

_____

_____

_____

_____

_____

_____

Lesson 3   Tom's day

1 Listen

Tick the word you hear.

a) live ☐   leave ☐
b) live ☐   leave ☐
c) live ☐   leave ☐
d) sit ☐   seat ☐
e) sit ☐   seat ☐
f) sit ☐   seat ☐

g) ship ☐   sheep ☐
h) ship ☐   sheep ☐
i) ship ☐   sheep ☐

2 Spelling

Find the *two* correct spellings.

return	retarn, return, returen, retrun, retern, returin, retturn, return
walk	wolk, walke, work, wark, walk, walek, valk, walk
stay	stai, stae, stey, istay, stay, satay, stay, saty
leave	leave, leeve, leive, live, laeve, leave, leav, leafe
rest	rast, rist, rest, reste, riste, rets, rest, reest
run	ran, run, runn, ren, rune, run, ron, ran
always	al ways, allways, alwaeys, always, alwais, always, allweys, all ways
shower	shwer, shower, showar, showre, shower, shover, shuwer, sower
after	aftr, after, afeter, ifter, aftre, efter, after, aftr
before	befor, befoer, befare, bifore, defore, before, beffor, before

3 Write

Put the words in the correct order.

a) always / drives / work / to / Hassan

_____

b) breakfast / has / Latifa / never

_____

c) the / sometimes / Ilham / in / watches / evening / television

_____

d) usually / rest / lunch /doesn't / Gamal / after

_____

e) a quarter / home / Murad / at / past / leaves / always / seven

_____

f) early / goes / my son / to / never / school

_____

4 Write

Join these sentences with **and then**.

a) Adnan gets up at seven o'clock. He has a shower.

_____

b) Jameela and Musa have breakfast at half past six. They go to school.

_____

c) I usually read after dinner. I go to bed.

_____

d) Tawfiq drives to work. He has breakfast in the canteen.

_____

e) Sarah gets dressed. She has her breakfast.

_____

f) We have dinner at seven o'clock. We go for a walk.

_____

g) Ahmed comes home at six. He has dinner with his family.

_____

h) The children finish school at one o'clock. They have lunch at home.

_____

5 Write

Write **do** or **does** in these questions.

a) When _____ Ahmed start work?

b) _____ Tom and Mary have lunch at home or at work?

c) At what time _____ school start?

d) What _____ you have for breakfast?

e) _____ Fatima usually stay at home in the evening?

f) _____ you go to bed early or late?

Write **don't** or **doesn't** in these sentences.

g) I _____ usually rest in the afternoon, I play football.

h) Simon _____ get up very early.

i) They _____ drive to work. They usually walk.

j) We _____ have a big breakfast. Just tea.

k) My brother-in-law _____ work in the morning. He starts work after lunch.

l) My car is old. It _____ usually start in the morning!

6 Dictation

Listen and write.

Fatima is talking about her younger sister.

_____

_____

_____

7 Read

Read about a taxi driver.

My uncle Rashid is a taxi driver in Amman. He always works very long hours. He usually works at night and so he gets up very late in the morning. He has a good breakfast and then he leaves home in his taxi. He usually drives to the airport first. He returns home at about two o'clock in the afternoon and has lunch with the family. After a short rest he gets back in his taxi and then drives to a hotel or to the bus station. Then he comes home very late. He says business is bad at the moment, but taxi drivers always say that!

Put a tick (✓) or a cross (X).

a) Rashid gets up late because he is lazy.
b) He doesn't usually have breakfast.
c) He has a rest after lunch.
d) In the afternoon he goes to a hotel or to the bus station.
e) Rashid says that business is quite good at the moment.

8 Write

Write about someone you know. Write about his day or her day.

_____

_____

_____

_____

1 Write

Write **always**, **never** and **every**.

We have Mathematics _____ Tuesday. I _____ understand anything and _____ get zero for homework!

2 Match

Match the words.

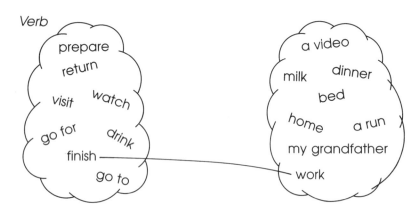

Verb

prepare
return
visit   watch
go for   drink
finish
go to

a video
milk   dinner
bed
home   a run
my grandfather
work

3 Punctuation

Write these sentences with punctuation and capital letters.

a)   i get up early every wednesday

_____

b)   salwa and noori usually stay at home on thursdays

_____

c)   do you usually have lunch at three oclock

_____

d)   peter works in a school in bahrain

_____

e)   we always visit my husbands aunt on mondays

_____

f)   when does ahmed usually have lunch

_____

g)   ill phone again on friday

_____

h)   farouq is a teacher but he doesnt teach english

_____

4   Find the word

Find the word that is different.

a)   go, run, walk, return, leave, have, come, drive
b)   cheese, eggs, milk, olives, bread, jam, toast
c)   March, June, September, January, Thursday, August, December
d)   week, July, month, year, hour, minute, day
e)   always, every, sometimes, usually, never
f)   when, why, how, what, white, why, where

5   Write

Write: **in, on** or **at**.

a)   I usually get up early _____ the summer.

b)   _____ Saturday afternoons I go for my driving lesson.

c)   We always have lunch _____ a quarter past two.

d)   My son, Fareed, was born _____ March _____ 1992.

e)   Ahmed doesn't like working _____ night.

f)   _____ the evening my wife and I usually go for a drive.

g)   I always stay _____ home in cold weather.

h)   I'll phone you _____ Tuesday.

i)   Let's go to the beach _____ the weekend.

j)   Peter is _____ holiday _____ the moment.

6 Listen and write

Fatima is talking about her week. Write the letters D, E, C, H and N on the timetable.

D = driving lesson, E = English class, C = computing, H = hospital, N = Najwa

	SATURDAY	SUNDAY	MONDAY	TUESDAY	WEDNESDAY	THURSDAY	FRIDAY
morning							
afternoon							
evening							

7 Write

Write about your week. First complete the timetable.

	SATURDAY	SUNDAY	MONDAY	TUESDAY	WEDNESDAY	THURSDAY	FRIDAY
morning							
afternoon							
evening							

Now write six sentences about your week. For example:

I always go to my English class on Tuesday evenings.

8 Match

Match the adjectives.

9 Crossword

Down

1 "What's Tariq's job?" "He's a —- .
He works for a big international
company." (11)
2 I like olives. They —- delicious! (3)
3 Latifa gets up early. Then —- has a
cup of tea. (3)
4 I leave home at eight o'clock and I
—- at five. (6)
7 I'd like that shirt, please. The —- on
the left. (3)
8 That's my book. Give —- to me. (2)
9 Miriam usually goes —- in Fahad As-
Salem Street on Thursdays. (8)
12 I study French —- Wednesday
evening. (5)
13 Ahmed likes —- at the refinery. (7)
18 Not early. (4)
20 "Is your car old?" "No, it isn't. It's —-
!" (3)
21 Peter goes to the market and then
—- has his driving lesson. (2)
23 What —- the food like in that restaurant? (2)

Across

1 The first meal of the day. (9 letters)
5 You are very noisy. Sit down and —-
quiet! (2)
6 I usually walk to work, but I —- go by
bus. (9)
10 My uncle starts work early —- the
morning. (2)
11 I hate yoghurt. I —- eat it. (5)
13 —- is that man over there? (3)
14

15

It's ... o'clock. (5)
16 "How are you?" "I'm —- , thanks!"
(1,1)
17 My sister-in-law is in hospital. She's
very —- .(3)
19 How —- children have you got? (4)
22 Ahmed sometimes works on the —-
shift. (5)
24 At the moment. (3)
25 I usually have tea, bread and two
—- in the morning. (4)

UNIT 6 On holiday

Lesson 1   **What's the weather like?**

1 Write

Write in the verbs: **rains, raining**.

> Look. It's _____ again.

> What terrible weather! It never _____ on Mars!

Look!

Noun	Adjective
sun	**sunny**
cloud	cloudy
wind	windy

The **sun** is very hot today.
The weather in summer is hot and **sunny**.

---

2 Spelling

Find the two correct spellings.

windy	windy, vindy, wandy, windi, windey, wendy, windy, vandy
raining	rainning, reining, rainign, raining, raining, ranning rayning, rainin
sunny	sunni, sanny, suny, sunny, sony, snny, zunny, sunny
cloudy	cloudy, cluody, celoudy, cloudi, cloody, clouby, cloudy, clody
holiday	holyday, holliday, holiday, holeday, holidy, holiday, holydey, hollidy
everyone	evryone, everyon, eviryone, evryoen, everyone, iveryone every one, everyone
terrible	tarrible, terribel, terible, terrible, terribl, terribal terrable, terrible
lovely	loveley, loveley, lovily, lovely, lovelly, lavely, lovely lovly,
yesterday	yisterday, yestrday, yesterday, yasterday, yesterday, yesterdy, yestarday

3 Write

Write in the verb. Choose the ending: **s, es** or (–).

a) Ahmed _____ in an oil refinery. (work)

b) We _____ in a flat near the market. (live)

c) Latifa usually _____ television in the evening. (watch)

d) I always _____ tea and toast for breakfast. (have)

e) Jamila and Mohsin _____ to primary school. (go)

f) It never _____ in Riyadh in the summer. (rain)

g) They always _____ late on holiday. (get up)

h) Jim _____ a lovely new car. (have)

i) Gamal _____ home at about half past seven. (return)

j) I sometimes _____ work at six o'clock in the morning. (start)

k) My sister and I _____ to school. (walk)

4 Punctuation

Write the sentences in their full form.

a) Today's a holiday.

_____

b) The weather's lovely.

_____

c) We're on holiday.

_____

d) They've got three children.

_____

e) I don't speak Arabic.

_____

f) It's raining.

_____

g) Ahmed doesn't work on holidays.

_____

h) Salwa's got a new job.

_____

i) I'll phone tomorrow.

_____

j) What's the weather like?

_____

k) I'm going for a swim.

_____

l) We haven't got a car.

_____

m) I'd like some cheese.

_____

5 Write

Put the words in the correct order.

a) sunny / yesterday / was / and / it / hot

_____

b) summer / like / in / the /what's / weather / ?

_____

c) always / it / January / does / in / rain / ?

_____

d) like / weather / don't / I / cold

_____

e) holiday / today / you / on / are / ?

_____

f) sometimes / in / Oman / summer / it / rains / in

_____

g) very / is / cold / winter / New York / in

_____

6 Read

Read Yacoub's letter to his English teacher in Doha.

Palace Hotel,
P.O. Box 763,
Istanbul,
Turkey.

23/2/95

Dear Mr Roberts,

How are you? I hope you and your family are well.

I'm here in Istanbul with my cousin. It's a very interesting city and I like it very much. There are a lot of people here from different countries. My cousin likes the bazaar, so we go there every day and look at the shops. There is something for everyone in the bazaar- clothes, gold, silver, food and carpets.

Istanbul is a nice place, but the weather is terrible It's cold and very windy. It's raining hard at the moment I think it rains here every day! Yesterday morning was quite sunny and so we went to the Topkapi Palace. We are going to the Blue Mosque this afternoon.

See you soon!

Best wishes

Yacoub Abdullah

Put a tick (✓) or a cross (X).

a) Yacoub is in Istanbul with his cousin.
b) He likes the city.
c) They visit the bazaar every day.
d) Yacoub likes the weather.
e) It is sunny now.
f) They are going to the Topkapi Palace this afternoon.

7 Write

Write to a friend in another country. Tell him or her about the weather.

(blank writing box)

Lesson 2   **What are you doing?**

1 Write

Put these verbs in the -ing form.

a) read _____ b) write _____

c) listen _____ d) study _____

e) speak _____ f) learn _____

g) look _____ h) think _____

2 Ask and answer

Ask five people

A

What're you doing?

B

I'm ... + ing

3 Write

Put the words in the correct order.

a)   doing / you / what / are / ?

_____

b)   like / weather / is / what / the / ?

_____

c)   do / you / where / live / ?

_____

d)   rain / in / it / winter / does / usually / the / ?

_____

e)   students / got / how / Peter / has / many / ?

_____

f)   do / hate / why / swimming / they / ?

_____

g)   born / you / when / were / ?

_____

h)   Khalid / work / when / start / does / ?

_____

4 Write

Write in the words: **to, for, at**

a) What are you waiting _____ ?

b) They are going _____ Alexandria by bus.

c) We always stay _____ home on Fridays.

d) Farouq usually goes _____ a walk in the evening.

e) I'm listening _____ the radio.

f) Look _____ Hassan! He's sleeping.

g) They are driving _____ the beach.

5 Dictation

Listen and write.

Hassan and his family are in Adhari Park.

6 Read

Put the verbs in the -ing form.

In the office

It is a busy morning in the office at AOC Limited. Fatima, Salwa and Mary (a) _____ (work) hard. Fatima (b)_____ (sit) at her desk. She (c) _____ (write) a letter on her computer. Salwa (d) _____ (speak) to Sulaiman. He is the boss and he is not very happy. He (e) _____ (go) to Riyadh tomorrow and he has a lot of work. On Mary's desk there are a lot of letters. She (f) _____ (read) one of the letters and she (g) _____ (drink) tea. At the door are two young men. They (h) _____ (wait) for Sulaiman.

7 Write

Look at the picture of Peter's classroom. Write sentences about the people.

| Peter | is | ... -ing |
| Omar and Tawfiq | are | |

_____

_____

_____

_____

_____

Lesson 3 — In a restaurant

1 Write

Write something, nothing, anything in the pictures.

There's _____ in the fridge.

Is there _____ good on television this evening?

There's _____ under that cupboard!

2 Spelling

Choose the right word.

a) Nadia is very _____ (quite / quiet) today. Do you think she is ill?

b) Fatima and Salwa are sitting in _____ (their / there) office.

c) Hamid is talking to his friends in the _____ (coffee / cafe).

d) Riyadh is a big city in the middle of a _____ (desert / dessert).

e) I like Cairo. It's an interesting _____ (palace / place).

f) Damascus is _____ (quite / quiet) cold in the winter.

g) _____ (their / there) are two mosques in the village.

h) What would you like for _____ (desert / dessert) - ice-cream or fruit?

i) I don't want anything, thank you - just a cup of _____ (coffee / cafe).

j) We are going to the royal _____ (palace / place) this afternoon.

3 Match

Match the words with the pictures: **soup, potatoes, fish, chocolate cake, vegetables, kebab, beefsteak**

4 Write

Write in these words: **salad, fruit, like, drink, afternoon, dessert, anything, water, kebab**

A: Good afternoon, sir.
B: Good (a) _____ .
A: What would you (b) _____ to eat?
B: Lamb (c) _____ .
A: (d) _____ with it?
B: Yes, rice and (e) _____ .
A: And for (f) _____ ?
B: What is there?
A: We've got ice-cream, and (g) _____ .
B: Fruit, please.
A: What would you like to (h) _____?.
B: Just (i) _____ .

5 Punctuation

Write out these sentences with punctuation and capital letters.

a)   it rains a lot in damascus in december

_____

b)   id like fish and rice please

_____

c)   whatre you doing

_____

d)   were waiting for hassan

_____

e)   salwas speaking to the boss

_____

f)   im going to abu dhabi on tuesday

_____

g)   whats the weather like in lebanon in summer

_____

h)   jamila and mohsin are very tired

_____

i)   saeeds taking photographs of bashir

_____

j)   mr smiths staying in the gulf hotel

_____

k)   theyre having lunch in the momtaz restaurant

_____

Present Continuous Tense

| to be | (not) | + | ... ing |

| I am | (not) | playing |

You are
He / She / It is
We are
They are

I'm waiting for a bus.
She's sitting near the door.
They are watching television.

I'm **not** waiting for a bus.
She is**n't** sitting near the door.
They are**n't** watching television.

6 Write

Write sentences using the verb in the Continuous form. For example:

Hamid **isn't working**, he's **resting** in his bedroom.

a) Jameel _____ (not study), he _____ (watch) televison.

b) I _____ (not sleep), I _____ (think)!

c) Khadija and Samia _____ (not go) the supermarket, they _____ (stay) at home.

d) Jim _____ (not play) tennis now, he _____ (work) in his office.

e) Salwa and her sister _____ (not cook), they _____ (speak) to Nadia in the sitting room.

f) Mohsin _____ (not listen) to the teacher, he _____ (read) a book.

g) We _____ (not wait) for a taxi, we _____ (rest) on the seat.

Look!

The Present Simple Tense

I	live	He	lives
You	(don't live)	She	(doesn't live)
We		It	
They			

7 Write

Put the verbs in the Present Simple form.

Tom and Mary (a) _____ (like) eating in restaurants. They (b) _____ (go) to a different restaurant every week. They usually (c) _____ (eat) Arabic or Turkish food. They sometimes (d) _____ (have) Indian or Pakistani food, but they (e) _____ (not like) very hot dishes.

Tom always (f) _____ (start) with meat or fish. He (g) _____ (not like) chicken. Mary (h) _____ (love) chicken, but she (i) _____ (not eat) lamb or beef. After that Tom usually (j) _____ (have) a dessert. Mary never (k) _____ (eat) sweet things, but she sometimes (l) _____ (have) fruit or cheese.

At the end of the meal they (m) _____ usually _____ (not drink) tea or coffee. They just (n) _____ (ask) the waiter for the bill!

Lesson 4   Where are you going?

1 Write

Write in the missing words.

Where are you _____?

We _____ going to Dubai.

_____ I come _____ you?

Of _____!

2 Match

Match the questions with the answers.

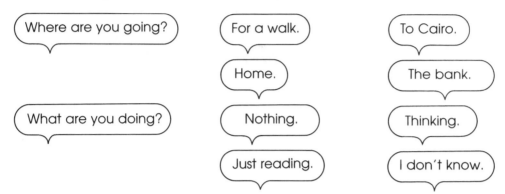

3 Find

Find the word that is different.

a) coming, going, waiting, evening, having, watching, driving
b) potatoes, vegetables, lamb, chicken, menu, salad
c) terrible, hot, weather, lovely, beautiful, cold, cloudy
d) coffee, water, juice, milk, cafe, tea
e) sit, stand, go, have, come, walk, run
f) in, on, do, between, next to, near, under

4 Match

Go in.   Go out.   Come in.   Come on.   Get in.   Get out.   Get up.

5 Write

Read about Khadija. Put the verbs in the right form. Use the Present Continuous (-ing) or the Present Simple tense.

Khadija is a teacher in a primary school. She always (a) _____ (get up) very early. She (b) _____ (pray) and then she (c) _____ (make) breakfast for the family. School (d) _____ (start) at half past eight and so she usually (e) _____ (leave) home at about eight o'clock. Her children (f) _____ (go) to school with her.

But today is a holiday. It is ten o'clock and Khadija is in the sitting room. She (g) _____ (have) coffee with some of her friends. The children (h) _____ (play) with their toys in the bedroom. They (i) _____ (make) a lot of noise.

Gamal, her husband, is on the phone. He (j) _____ (talk) to his brother-in-law, Abdul Rahim. On holidays they usually (k) _____ (go) for a picnic with Abdul Rahim. They (l) _____ (drive) to the desert and (m) _____ (cook) lamb and rice. But today the weather is bad. It (n) _____ (rain), and so Gamal (o) _____ (ask) Abdul Rahim and his family to come to their house for lunch.

6 Write

Write out these sentences in the short forms. Example:

I am waiting for a bus. **I'm** waiting for a bus.

a) We would like some sandwiches. _____

b) They have got six children. _____

c) We are making some Turkish coffee. _____

d) The weather is not very good today. _____

e) Rashid does not like driving. _____

f) You are not listening to me! _____

g) Mustapha has got two horses. _____

h) I have not got your telephone number. _____

i) The boys do not speak English. _____

j) The driver is waiting near the hotel. _____

k) I am not from Cairo. _____

7 Crossword

Across

1 The — today is terrible. (7 letters)
5 Listen and — . (3)
7

He is sleeping — the tree. (5)
9 I'm = — (1,2)
10 Today is National Day. Everyone is — holiday. (2)
11 Tom and Mary usually — in a restaurant every week. (3)
12 Do not = — (4)
13 It — rains in Riyadh in the summer. (5)
14

He's — the window. (7)
18 "I'm going to the beach?" "Are you? — I come with you?" (3)

Down

20 It's a terrible day. It's cold and very — (5)
22 "My address is — Box 149" (2)
23 "I'm going to the airport." "OK. — in please." (3)
25 1,000,000 = a — (7)
27 When does this shop — ? (4)

Down

1 What — you like to drink? (5)
2 Salwa is standing near the office window — talking to Fatima. (3)
3 That's Latifa's handbag. Give it to — .(3)
4 Oh look at the weather! It's — again. (7)
5 "I'd like chicken with vegetables and rice."
  "Yes, I'd like the — , please." (4)
6 Today is Sunday. — was Saturday. (9)
8

She's — an orange (6)
15 This is a nice — for a picnic. (5)
16 "Are you going to the hospital?"
  "— , I'm not. I'm going to the university." (2)
17

19 "Where are you going?" "I'm going — I'm tired." (4)
21

23

24 Miriam likes listening — music. (2)
26 We always go to the mountains — July. (2)

Appendix — مُلْحَق

Grammatical terms	مُصْطَلَحات نَحْوِيَّة
noun	الاسْم
countable noun	إِسْم قابِل للعَدّ
uncountable noun	إِسْم غير قابِل للعَدّ
pronoun	الضَّمير
subject pronoun	ضَمير الفاعِل
object pronoun	ضَمير المَفْعول
Present simple tense	صيغة المُضارِع البَسيط
Present continuous tense	صيغة المُضارِع المُسْتَمِرّ
Past simple	الماضي البَسيط
Examples	أَمْثِلَة
biscuit	بَسْكَويت
chair	كُرْسِيّ
water	ماء
juice	عَصير
she	هِيَ
it	هُوَ، هِيَ (غير العاقِل)
them	هُما، هُمْ، هُنَّ
I	أنا
you	أَنْتَ، أَنْتِ
he	هُوَ
she	هِيَ
me	...ي
you	...لَكَ
him	...ه
her	...ها
I study English	أَتَعَلَّم الإِنْكِليزِيَّة
I am studying English	أَتَعَلَّم الإِنْكِليزِيَّة حالِيًّا
I was	كُنْت
You were	كُنْت
He was	كان

A

accountant	مُحاسِب
address	عُنْوان
Africa	أَفْريقيا
after	بَعْد...
also	أَيْضًا
always	دائِمًا
animal	حَيَوان
another	آخَر
anything	أيُّ شَيْء
apartment	شَقَّة
April	نَيْسان (أبريل)
Arabic	العَرَبِيَّة
arm	ذِراع
at home	في المَنْزِل
at night	في اللَّيْل
at work	في العَمَل
August	آب (أغسطس)

B

bargain	صَفْقَة
bath	حَمّام
beach	شاطِئ
beans	فاصوليا
because	لأَنَّ...
bed	سَرير
bee	نَحْلَة
beef	لَحْمُ بَقَر
beefsteak	شَريحَةُ لَحْم بَقَرِيّ
before	قَبْل...
Be quiet!	اِلْزَمِ الهُدوءَ!
birth (date of birth)	وِلادَة (تاريخُ الوِلادَة)
birthday	عيدُ ميلاد
biscuit	بَسْكَويت
boat	مَرْكَب
boring	مُمِلّ
to be born	وُلِدَ

both	كِلا، كِلْتا
bread	خُبْز
breakfast	طَعامُ الفَطور
Britain	بَريطانْيا
brother-in-law	أخو الزَّوج أو الزَّوجَة
bus driver	سائِقُ الباص
business man	رَجُلُ أعْمال
business woman	سَيِّدَةُ أعْمال
by	قُرْبَ...

C

cab	سَيّارَةُ أُجْرَة
café	مَقْهى
cake	كَعْكَة
called	مَدْعُوّ
camel	جَمَل
a can of...	عُلْبَةُ...
Can I have...?	هَلْ يُمْكِنُني أنْ أحْصُلَ عَلى...؟
Can I see...?	هَلْ يُمْكِنُني أنْ أرَى...؟
Canada	كَنَدا
Canadian	كَنَديّ
cap	قُبَّعَة
carpet	سَجّادَة
cashier	أمينُ صُنْدوق
cat	هِرّ
to catch	أمْسَكَ بِـ
centre	وَسَط
certificate	شَهادَة
cheese	جُبْن
chicken	دَجاجَة
chocolate	شوكولا
cigarette	سيجارَة
class	صَفّ
clean	نَظيف
clever	ماهِر
to close	أغْلَقَ
clothes	مَلابِسُ

cloud	سَحابَة
coat	مِعْطَف
cola	كولا
college	كُلِّيَّة
colour	لَوْن
to come from	كانَ مِنْ (بَلَد...)
Come in!	أُدْخُلي/أُدْخُلْ
Come on!	هَيّا!
commercial	تِجاريّ
Congratulations!	تَهانينا!
cooking	طَبْخ
to cost	كَلَّفَ
cup	كوب

D

danger	إنْتَبِهْ، خَطَرْ!
dangerous	خَطِر
date	بَلَحَة
date of birth	تاريخُ الوِلادَة
daughter-in-law	كَنَّة (زَوْجَةُ الابْن)
December	كانون الأوَّل (ديسمبر)
delicious	شَهِيّ
desert	صَحْراءُ
dessert	حَلْوى (بَعْدَ الطَّعام)
dictionary	قاموس
different	مُخْتَلِف
difficult	صَعْب
dinner	طَعامُ العَشاء
diploma	شَهادَة
dish	صَحْن
district	مُقاطَعة
to do	قامَ بِـ
What do you do?	ما هِيَ مِهْنَتُك؟
What are you doing?	ماذا تَفْعَلُ الآنَ؟
document	وَثيقَة
dog	كَلْب
dress	ثَوْب

drink	شَراب
to drink	شَرِبَ
to drive	قادَ
driving licence	رُخْصَةُ سَوْق

E

each	كُلّ
early	باكِرًا
easy	سَهْل
to eat	أَكَلَ
eggs	بَيْض
elephant	فيل
engineer	مُهَنْدِس
enough	كافٍ
envelope	ظَرْف
every	كُلّ
everyone	كُلُّ شَخْص
excellent	مُمْتاز

F

factor	عامِل
famous	شَهير
fantastic	خارِق
far	بَعيد
farming	زِراعَة
fast	سَريع
father-in-law	حَمو (أَبو الزَّوْجَة أو الزَّوْج)
February	شُباط (فبراير)
filing cabinet	خِزانة المِلَفّات
to finish	أَنْهَى
fish	سَمَكَة
to fish	إصْطادَ السَّمَكَ
fishing	صَيْدُ السَّمَك
flat	مُسَطَّح
food	طَعام
footballer	لاعِبُ كُرَة قَدَم
free time	وَقْتُ فَراغ

funny	مُضْحِك

G

garden	حَديقَة
gardening	الاعْتِناء بالحَديقة
gate	بَوّابَة
to get up	نَهَضَ
to get dressed	إرْتَدَى مَلابِسَه
to get in	دَخَلَ
to get out	خَرَجَ
Geography	الجُغْرافيا
to give	أَعْطَى
glass	زُجاج
to go	ذَهَبَ
to go for (a walk, a run)	ذَهَبَ (لِيَتَمَشَّى أو لِيَرْكُضَ)
goat	عَنْزَة
gold	ذَهَبٌ
goodbye	وَداعًا
good idea	فِكْرَة حَسَنة
grass	عُشْب
great	عَظيم
guard	حارِس
guest	ضَيْف
Gulf	الخَليج

H

half	نِصْف
half past...	... والنِّصْف
hard	صُلْب
hat	قُبَّعَة (عَسْكَريَّة)
to hate	كَرِهَ
Have a seat	تَفَضَّلي بالجُلوس!
to have	عِنْدَهُ...
to have (breakfast, a shower)	تَناوَلَ (الفَطورَ)؛ أَخَذَ (حَمّامًا)
to have got	عِنْدَه...
Help yourself!	تَفَضَّلي!

her	ها ...
Here you are!	تَفَضَّلْ
him	... ه
History	التّاريخ
hobby	هِوايَة
holiday	يَوْمُ عُطْلَة
home	بَيْت
homework	فَرْض مَنْزِليّ
honey	عَسَل
horrible	رَهيب
horse	حِصان

I

I'd like (I would like)	أَرْغَبُ في ...
identification card	بِطاقَةُ تَعْريف
in the morning (afternoon/evening)	في الصَّباح (بَعْد الظُّهْر/ في المَساء)
India	الهِنْد
Indian	هِنْديّ
interesting	مُمْتِع
intermediate school	مَدْرَسَة مُتَوَسِّطة
international	دَوْليّ
it's a bargain!	اِتَّفَقْنا!
it's too much!	هٰذا كَثير!
I was born...	وُلِدْتُ ...

J

jam	مُرَبّى
January	كانون الثّاني (يناير)
juice	عَصير
July	تَمّوز (يوليو)
June	حَزيران (يونيو)
just	تَمامًا

K

kebab	كَباب (لَحم مَشْويّ)
kind	نَوْع

L

lake	بُحَيْرَة
lamb	حَمَل
language	لُغَة
large	واسِع
Last price!	هٰذا هو السِّعْر النِّهائيّ!
later	لاحِقًا
lazy	كَسول
to learn	تَعَلَّم
learning	تَعَلُّم
to leave	غادَرَ
lecturer	مُحاضِر
lesson	دَرْس
Let's... (Let us)	هَيّا بِنا ...
letter	رِسالة
licence	تَرْخيص
to like	أَحَبّ
list	قائِمَة
to listen (to)	أَصْغى إلى ...
a little	قَليل ...
to live	عاشَ
locker	خِزانَة
to look (at)	نَظَرَ إلى
lot (a lot of)	عَدَد وافِر مِن ...
to love	أَحَبَّ
lovely	مُحَبَّب
lunch	طَعامُ الغَداء

M

main gate	البَوّابَة الرَّئيسيّة
to make	صَنَعَ
March	آذار (مارس)
Mathematics	الرِّياضِيّات
May	أَيّار (مايو)
meal	وَجْبَة (طَعامٍ)
meat	لَحْم
menu	قائِمَةُ الطَّعام

me	ي . . .	**P**	
me too	أَنا أَيْضًا	Pakistan	الباكِسْتان
Middle East	الشَّرق الأَوْسَط	Pakistani	باكِسْتانيّ
milk	حَليب	paper	وَرَقَة
million	مِلْيون	party	حَفْلَة
money	مال	pass	إذْن المُرور
monkey	قِرْد	pea	بِسِلّى
more	أَكْثَرُ	peach	خَوْخ
mother-in-law	حَماة (أُمُّ الزَّوْج أَو الزَّوْجة)	permit	رُخْصَة
must	يَجِبُ	photograph	صورَة فوتوغرافيَّة
		picnic	نُزْهَة
N		pink	وَرْديّ
news reader	مُذيعُ الأَخْبار	place	مَكان
never	أَبَدًا	to play	لَعِبَ
night shift	نَوْبَةُ العَمَل لَيْلًا	playing	لَعِبٌ
No entry	مَمْنوع الدُّخول!	P.O. Box	صُنْدوقُ البَريد
noisy	ضاجّ	potato	بَطاطا
No parking	مَمْنوع وُقوفُ السَّيّارات!	pound	رَطْل إنْكليزيّ
No smoking	مَمْنوع التَّدْخين!	it's pouring	المَطَرُ يَهْطل بغَزارة
note	وَرَقَة نَقْديَّة	to pray	تَوَسَّلَ إلى
nothing	لا شَيْء	to prepare	أَعَدَّ
not much	لَيْسَ كَثيرًا	price	سِعْر
November	تِشْرين الثَّاني (نوفمبر)	primary school	مَدْرَسَة ابْتِدائيَّة
O		**Q**	
October	تِشْرين الأَوَّل (أكتوبر)	quarter	رُبْع
of course	طَبْعًا	question	سُؤال
oil	زَيْت	quiet	هادِئ
older	أَكْبَرُ سِنًّا		
olives	زَيْتون	**R**	
the one...	الَّذي، الَّتي . . .	to rain	أَمْطَرَتِ (السَّماءُ)
on holiday	في عُطْلَة	to read	قَرَأَ
on Friday	نَهارَ الجُمْعَة	reading	قِراءَة
to open	فَتَحَ	really	حَقًّا
out of order	غَيْرُ صالِح لِلاسْتِعْمال	refinery	مِصْفاة (نَفْط)
overalls	رِداء سِرْواليّ	to rest	إرْتاحَ
		to return	عادَ

ring	حَلْقَة	to speak	تَكَلَّمَ
Riyal	ريال	sports car	سَيَّارَة رياضِيَّة
run	رَكْضٌ	stamp	طابَع بَريدِيّ
to run	رَكَضَ	to stand up	وَقَفَ
		to start	بَدَأَ
S		to stay	بَقِيَ
the same	نَفْسُه	steward	مُضيف
to say	قالَ	stewardess	مُضيفَة
science	عِلْم	to study	دَرَسَ
sea	بَحْر	subject	مَوْضوع
secondary school	مَدْرَسَة ثانَوِيَّة	suburb	ضاحِية
security guard	رَجُلُ أَمْن	sugar	سُكَّر
see (can I see...?)	رَأَى (هَل يُمْكِنُني أَنْ أَرَى . . . ؟)	suit	بَذْلَة
See you later!	أَراكَ لاحِقًا!	summer	الصَّيْف
See you soon!	إلى اللِّقاء!	sunny	مُشْمِس
September	أَيْلول (سبتمبر)	supermarket	مَتْجر كَبير (سوبرماركت)
shelf	رَفّ	sure (I'm not sure)	واثِق (لَسْتُ واثِقًا)
shirt	قَميص	sweet	حُلْو
shoes	زَوْجُ أَحْذِيَة	swing	تَأَرْجُح
shopping	تَسَوُّق	to swim	سَبَحَ
to show	عَرَضَ	swimming	سِباحَة
Show me...	أَرِني . . .		
shower	وابِل مِنَ المَطَر	**T**	
silver	فِضَّة	to take (a photograph)	اِلْتَقَطَ (صورَةً)
sister-in-law	أُخْتُ الزَّوْج أو الزَّوْجَة	to teach	عَلَّمَ
to sit	جَلَسَ	tennis	كُرَةُ المَضْرِب
to sit down	قَعَدَ	terrible	رَديء
skirt	تَنّورَة	Thailand	تايلانْدا
to sleep	نامَ	then (and then...)	ثُمَّ
slow	خَفِّف سَيْرَكَ!	to think	فَكَّرَ
snake	حَيَّة	tiger	نَمِر
some	بَعْض	toast	خُبْز مُحَمَّص
some more	المَزيد مِن . . .	trader	تاجِر
something	شَيْء ما	trading	مُتاجَرَة
sometimes	أَحْيانًا	transport	نَقْل
son-in-law	صِهْر (زَوْجُ الابْنَة)	trousers	سَراويلُ
soup	حَساء	too	أَيْضًا